PAPERISTS

Infinite Possibilities
in Paper Art

SANDU

PAPERISTS

Infinite Possibilities
in Paper Art

First published in 2021 by Sandu Publishing Co., Ltd.

Sponsored by Design 360° — Concept & Design Magazine
Edited and produced by Sandu Publishing Co., Ltd.
Book design, concepts & art direction by Sandu Publishing Co., Ltd.

info@sandupublishing.com
www.sandupublishing.com
weibo.com/sandupublishing
Address: 5th Floor, Wah Kit Commercial Centre,
302 Des Voeux Road Central, Hong Kong

Publisher: Sandu Publishing Co., Ltd.
Chief Editor: Wang Shaoqiang
Executive Editor: July Wu
Copy Editor: Gingko Press
Designers: Wu Yanting, Su Zhenhua, Huang Zhiyi, Liu Xian

Cover projects by Ale Rambar, Diana Beltran Herrera,
Estudio Guardabosques, Hazel Glass, Héloïse Bossard, Jackie Wen,
JUDiTH+ROLFE, María Laura Benavente Sovieri, Matt Shlian,
Owen Gildersleeve, Pippa Dyrlaga, Sara Rayo, Shinobu Ohashi,
Sota, Tania Lissova, Yulia Brodskaya, Zai Divecha, Zim&Zou
Cover Design: Wu Yanting

Size: 190 mm × 250 mm
First Edition: 2021

ISBN: 978-988-74492-7-0

Printed and bound in China

CONTENTS

PREFACE

The Hidden Power of Paper

By Hazel Glass

It can be smooth or textured. It can be made thick and opaque as a board or thin and sheer as an insect wing. Its hues can be dyed, painted, inked, stained, and bleached. Its fibers can be cut, torn, burned, embossed, engraved, creased, folded, rolled, glued, molded, and carved. You might find it in sheets as large as a wall or itty bitty scraps like confetti.

Paper can be and do all these things and many more, yet most people overlook it. We are so used to handing it over as currency for a cup of coffee, stapling it together as a work document, or seeing it fly as a child's toy airplane, that we forget we are holding the incredible potential for art in our hands. From newspapers, envelopes, and movie tickets to coffee filters, toilet paper, and lunch sacks, paper has often been seen as a disposable item in recent centuries. As a material, it is used only briefly and then tossed out, burned as fuel, or recycled. Its value is fleeting.

Even throughout the history of paper art, this is so. *Noshi*, a form of *origami*, is used in gift-wrapping; Papel Picado (perforated paper) is made from tissue and hung in the streets of Mexico, exposed to the weather; Piñatas, made of paper pieces, are smashed with sticks as a part of a ceremony; in China, paper cuts are glued to the exteriors of windows, as mere fleeting decorations; Wycinanki, a Slavic form of paper cutting traditionally done with sheep shears, is pasted on roof beams to gather dust; gorgeous, intricate patterns are cut to make paper stencils for dyeing textiles in Japan, which are thrown out after each *kimono* (a traditional Japanese dress). The works preserved in museums are more typically paintings on canvas or panel, and sculptures in metal or stone. There are some photographs, some ink or charcoal drawings, but in general, paper is just a surface underneath the world of art. It is a vessel for the printed word, the watercolor painting or the glossy advertisement, only valued for what it carries. It is only seen as a vacant base upon which the true worth is built, often serving as the backdrop, rarely the star.

However, paper being so often underestimated gives paper artists a distinct advantage. While the majority of artists are using the celebrated slab of clay or loaded brush to express themselves creatively, we turn to the inconspicuous piece of paper. Those classical artists begin their quest for extraordinary compositions by following in the footsteps of the masters. They study known techniques, building their skills elbow to elbow with the crowd. They trudge down packed creative highways, struggling to find a stylistic turn off that will help them stand apart. Nonetheless, the landscape is choked with the tangled metropolitan intersections of custom.

Meanwhile, with so few paths previously worn, we stand before a "paper art wilderness" brimming with uncharted territory. We can follow our creative whims and wander for days on end without stumbling over another's trail. Walking in whichever style or direction we wish, at whatever pace, we are more able to forge our own unique paths than fall into the ruts of tradition. This gives us room to grow, to experiment, and to develop new methods of expression. We can establish personal design foundations with panoramic views and far-reaching visions, before carrying on with our boundary-pushing voyage across this lush and neglected land.

My journey to explore paper art, though brief and tiny in the face of paper art's history, has led me to places I would never have dreamed of. I began with symmetrical decorative designs, focusing my energy on the technical challenges of cutting paper. This led to more organic forms, where I pushed the complexity of my color palettes. From there, I did a study in-depth, turning my work into a sculptural form. Now I meander between the deep forests and sweeping seascapes of my otherworldly landscapes, between clean and stylized ornate symbolism and the abstracted patterns of nature, wearing byways between them to better connect everything that I have learned moving forward.

And this is all within my particular region of layered paper cutting. There are dozens of paper art domains, where creative voyagers are blazing their own trails, using unexpected tools and bridging concepts across borders. Paper, a kind of material that is mostly viewed as dull and rudimentary, becomes elegant and sophisticated in the hands of a paper artist—revolutionary and inspiring. We can see their towering ideas as beacons across the valley, and as it happens in art, others are beginning the pilgrimage to their realm.

These new roads bring a special sort of delight to viewers, as they encounter the unexpected. We know that this material is the same as the one we use to package pasta or even blow our nose, yet here it comes, taking on a magical transformation that art gifts every material. It is only paper. But it is becoming giant textural tapestries, collaged portraits, delicate sheets of lace, flowing quilled decorations, layered illustrations, folded-sheet fashion, carved book sculptures, elaborate *origami* installations, confetti mosaics, and miniature silhouettes… There are not adequate names for the styles and techniques applied to paper art because we keep creating something new as we go along the journey. It is a journey filled with adventure, exploration, and exciting new scenery. We don't know what is around the next bend in the road. But isn't that the best part of a voyage?

"Paper, a kind of material that is mostly viewed as dull and rudimentary, becomes elegant and sophisticated in the hands of a paper artist—revolutionary and inspiring."

JUDiTH+ROLFE

"Depicting flora in my paper artwork connects us to nature when we're unable to be in the natural world physically."

JUDiTH+ROLFE is a studio currently based in Saint Paul, Minnesota. On-edge paper is primarily used to create their intricate and unique artwork, but some pieces also incorporate techniques such as folding, cutting, and layering. Flora, geometry, and architecture are constant themes in their work.

Chrysanthemum

The chrysanthemum was selected as the subject for its symbolism and spirituality, as well as its assortment of colors.

Tools: *Craft blade, tweezers, glue*
Techniques: *Unmounted on-edge paper, gluing*

When and how did you start your journey of paper art?

My paper art journey started in 2016. Prior to that, Rolfe and I were living and working as architects in New York City. A job opportunity arose for Rolfe, which subsequently brought us to Minnesota. I knew I needed a change from architecture, but I had no clue what else I wanted to do, except working with my hands. One day, after a fruitless search for personalized name gifts, I decided to make some myself. Using pre-cut paper strips, I started rolling paper coils and arranged them to form names. I fell in love with the process, and have been working with paper almost every day since then. A few years later, we are still on this exciting journey.

Could you briefly describe your process of creating a paper artwork?

I create dimensional paper artwork using various techniques such as folding, cutting, and layering. However, my preferred technique is working with strips of paper set on edge, which can broadly be called "quilling." Traditional quilling or paper filigree work consists of rolled paper strips manipulated into various decorative shapes which are then used to compose an image. Instead of using the decorative shapes typically associated with quilling, I treat each strip of paper as a line of the image. The paper strip is still kept on its edge and glued down individually to the background panel, or to each other, to create the artwork.

Flowers and plants are one of the main themes of your artworks, why do you enjoy depicting them so much?

Nature is universal and essential. As human beings, even though our society is becoming detached from the natural world, we can still appreciate its beauty. We all have this innate desire and need for nature, as evidenced by how good we feel when we're in it. Depicting flora in my paper artwork connects us to nature when we're unable to be in the natural world physically.

In the process of creating an artwork, which part do you enjoy the most?

My favorite part is when I get into the flow state and am fully immersed in the work. The repetitive nature of cutting, shaping, and gluing paper becomes meditative and relaxing, which allows me to completely focus on the task at hand.

You have done a lot of commissioned projects as well as personal artworks. What are the differences when you are creating these two kinds of projects?

A successful commission piece is a true collaboration between the client and the artist. I definitely get more stressed out when working on a commissioned piece compared to a personal work because I have to consider the client's preferences. However, the client may come up with ideas and combinations that I might never have thought of, which challenges me to step outside of my comfort zone to try something different occasionally.

Are there any paper artists that you are especially fond of? What have you learned from them?

There are many paper artists who I admire and have been inspired by, but I consider Yulia Brodskaya to be one of the best paper artists specializing in on-edge paper art. Yulia's work made me realize the possibilities of this art form, and her work inspired me to try creating my own paper art in the first place. I began to appreciate that "quilling" doesn't have to be relegated to a hobby or craft. Instead, it can be elevated to the realm of fine art, just like painting or sculpture.

What is the biggest difference between your recent works and those you created in the beginning?

My work has come a long way since those days when I created personalized name works made out of paper coils. I think my skills are constantly improving and evolving. There is more focus on the composition and design of a canvas, rather than the re-creation of a single element. Recently, I've been working on larger-scale pieces as well as installations, both of which are projects I wouldn't have had the confidence to do in the beginning.

Poppies, Freesia

"Poppies" and "Freesia" were inspired by *ikebana*, the Japanese art of flower arrangement, with their lines and forms guiding the composition of the work. Due to their long stems and minimalist arrangement, these two floral pieces unexpectedly made for a fitting diptych.

Tools: *Craft blade, tweezers, glue*
Techniques: *On-edge paper, gluing*

Ginkgo No. 2, Ginkgo No. 4, Ginkgo No. 5, Horse Chestnut

These four pieces are part of the overlapping leaf series, inspired by the changing colors of fall foliage and falling autumn leaves. This series is an ongoing investigation into composition within a square canvas. Negative spaces where the leaves intersect allow for the paper colors reflect and bounce off the white background, to create breathing room from the dense intricacy of the leaf "veins."

Tools: *Craft blade, tweezers, glue*
Techniques: *On-edge paper, gluing*

Morning Glory

The vibrancy and beautiful trumpet-shaped blooms of the morning glory are captured in this piece. The color gradient in the center of the flower is achieved by using graduated color quilling paper that fades to white, contrasting with the darker colors of the surrounding petals.

Tools: *Craft blade, tweezers, glue*
Techniques: *On-edge paper, gluing*

◂ **Bearded Iris**

▴ **Stargazer Lily**

These two artworks were commissioned pieces with the flower choice, layout, and colors determined by the clients' preferences. The clients were given a few sketches to choose from, and their comments helped guide the direction of the artwork.

Tools: *Craft blade, tweezers, glue*
Techniques: *On-edge paper, gluing*

▲ Magnolia

This magnolia piece was an experiment to see if a larger flower could be made using the "unmounted" technique.

Tools: *Craft blade, tweezers, glue*
Techniques: *Unmounted on-edge paper, gluing*

▸ Lotus

This bloom was created by gluing ten-millimeter paper strips simply to each other rather than a backing material. Remarkably, the paper strips are sturdy and robust enough to be picked up by hand.

Tools: *Craft blade, tweezers, glue*
Techniques: *Unmounted on-edge paper, gluing*

Dahlias

There are a great number of Dahlia varieties, this floral piece was based on the award-winning Dahlia called "Café au Lait," cream-colored blooms tinged with peachy-pink blush highlights.

Tools: *Craft blade, tweezers, glue*
Techniques: *On-edge paper, gluing*

Shinobu Ohashi

"Paper cutting is more like 'subtraction' while painting is 'addition.' It is an art of removing."

Shinobu Ohashi started her career as a *kirie* (paper cutting) artist in 2008 in her junior year at university. Using black paper and hand-tinted Japanese rice paper, she works on paper cutting to evoke the beauty of stained glass. She weaves together motifs like words and music with the images of birds and plants in her compositions.

桜始開

Kusa wo Musubu

Meaning "tie the grass," this seamless piece is made of repeated motifs of poisonous herbs. It is created for producing *furoshiki*, a Japanese cloth for packing gifts and the like.

Tools: *Design knife, Japanese paper, watercolor, glue*
Techniques: *Painting, cutting, gluing*

Interview with **Shinobu Ohashi**

When and how did you start your journey with paper art? Could you briefly describe your creative process?

The first time I met paper cutting was in elementary school when I found paper cutting illustrations in the textbooks. However, my main focus of art at that time was painting, so I didn't pay much attention to it. At the age of 14, I realized that my paintings had no personality. Suddenly, the childhood memory of paper cutting came to me, and I decided to try this artistic approach of expression and go on a creative journey with it. In my opinion, paper cutting is more like "subtraction" while painting is "addition." It is an art of removing, and I am fascinated by how the artwork gradually becomes visible.

I usually draft on black paper and cut along the lines. Then I tint the Japanese paper with watercolor paint and paste the colored pieces on the cutouts to simulate the beauty of stained glass.

What do you want to express through your artworks? Where do you usually get inspiration?

At first glance, my artwork may seem colorful and bright, but it is not. The main concept of my paper cutting is "sorrow," but I am careful not to express that directly and explicitly.

For inspiration, old novels, music, and traveling are helpful to me. Since I have synesthesia, I can feel the music, shapes, colors, and texts with layouts of design popping up in my head. Due to these perceptions, I haven't experienced a creative block luckily. Yet, my life is sometimes hindered by them. For instance, walking around the city tires my brain and body because sounds keep flashing through my mind along the way.

How did you find your style on paper art?

When I started my journey of paper cutting, most of the artists' work was completed with black construction paper. Thinking of ways to expand the range of expression, I decided to add colors to my artworks. At the age of 14, I colored a sheet of white drawing paper with watercolor paints and laid it underneath the cutout of black drawing paper. Further, I replaced white drawing paper with Japanese paper which made more delicate expressions possible.

Cut-out words aren't seen very often in paper art. How did you come up with the idea of cutting words out of paper and how do you combine the patterns and fonts harmoniously?

The idea also came from synesthesia. I can feel the phrases and sentences floating in the air and want to share it with someone. *Kanji* is relatively easy to express due to its solid form. Yet, *hiragana* (Japanese syllabary) is a little difficult to cut since the lines are often separated instead of connected. When fonts become part of my artworks, I try to read them and do calculations to draw lines to make them look natural.

Most of your artworks involve flowers. Why are they so attractive to you?

I like flowers because of floriography. I don't like to make artworks without meanings. By depicting flowers with special meanings, I am able to convey a secret emotion and message through my artworks.

Is there anything new that you would like to try, or is there anything that you are working on and hope to improve?

I want to make videos about my artworks, especially those incorporating fonts, though I haven't decided which technology to use. Besides, since Japan is small, it is easy for someone to imitate others. Therefore, I think it important to make unique work that no one can copy. To achieve this, I need to improve my skills and sense of beauty.

Hisureba Hana

Written in *kanji* as " 秘すれば花 ," this piece is a wordplay of a Japanese saying that goes: "If you keep it secret, it will be a flower." Instead of the real flower planted in the soil, the "flower" symbolizes "beauty" or "aesthetics," meaning that the real beauty of art is sometimes hidden and becomes more attractive being a secret.

Tools: *Design knife, Japanese paper, watercolor, glue*
Techniques: *Painting, cutting, gluing*

Himitsu no Murasaki

Meaning "the secret of purple," this piece is inspired by the beautiful purple of the cocktail "Violet Fizz." With a white pigeon carrying a key to unlock a lock, it has the meaning of sharing secrets.

Tools: *Design knife, Japanese paper, watercolor, glue*
Techniques: *Painting, cutting, gluing*

Geshi

Geshi, written in *kanji* as "夏至," means "summer solstice." The round frame of the piece resembles the starry sky in summer, and the orange flowers are Chinese trumpet vines.

Tools: *Design knife, Japanese paper, watercolor, glue*
Techniques: *Painting, cutting, gluing*

Hana Monogatari

Written in *kanji* as " 花物語 " which means "the story of flower," this piece is inspired by a sad story about a sunflower in ancient Japanese literature. By cutting "paper" (a sheet of the manuscript) out of paper, Shinobu injected some playfulness into the piece.

Tools: *Design knife, Japanese paper, watercolor, glue*
Techniques: *Painting, cutting, gluing*

Kahen no Wa wo Kaku

Written in *kanji* as " 花片の輪をかく " which means "to draw a petal ring," this piece was created for decorating the windows of a coffee shop, with two white pigeons flying near and Lantana flowers blooming.

Tools: *Design knife, Japanese paper, watercolor, glue*
Techniques: *Painting, cutting, gluing*

▲ Suimu no Yubikiri

Through "Suimu no Yubikiri" (water dreams and promises), Shinobu aimed to carry the Hydrangea flowers floating on the river, with lines cut out of paper performing the water surface and the shadow acting as part of the artwork. Besides, the small rabbit rowing a small boat is an allusion to the fairy tale "Thumbelina."

Tools: *Design knife, Japanese paper, watercolor, glue*
Techniques: *Painting, cutting, gluing*

► Hasunuma Onsen

This piece is dedicated to the "Hasunuma Onsen," written in *kanji* as " はすぬま温泉 ," a theme bathhouse in Kamata, Tokyo, using the windows and decorations of the building as the motifs.

Tools: *Design knife, Japanese paper, watercolor, glue*
Techniques: *Painting, cutting, gluing*

Hazel Glass

"What keeps me coming back to paper art is the process of cutting. It is a tranquil moment, a form of meditation for me to empty my mind and follow the flow of the line."

Having spent two decades as a self-taught artist, **Hazel Glass** has always followed her own path. While paper cutting art is often white and a single sheet, she works instead with color and multiple layers, creating interwoven contrast and a strata of depth. Her sources of inspiration range from traditional decorative design and fairy tales to organic patterns in nature.

The Fall of Day

This piece was born from travels in the American Southwest desert. Though mostly barren rock, it is also bejeweled with pristine and still lakes that mirror the famously vivid sunsets and fiery sculpted canyons.

Tools: *Craft knife, archival glue, rivets*
Techniques: *Drawing, cutting, layering, gluing, riveting*

How long does it take you to create a piece of paper art on average?

It takes me a day to a month to create, depending on how complex the design is, how intricate the cutting is, and how many layers the piece has. The part that I spend the most time on is the palette. Color plays an essential role in my art, so finding the perfect fit for a piece involves a lot of consideration.

In the process of creating an artwork, which part do you enjoy the most?

What keeps me coming back to paper art is the process of cutting. It is a tranquil moment, a form of meditation for me to empty my mind and follow the flow of the line. All the anxieties of the world dissolve, and there is nothing left but my knife and the paper.

Why is paper art special to you compared with other forms of art?

Every artist knows the sensation of picking up a new tool, and the feeling that the tool will result in something special. I knew that sensation the first time when I cut a sheet of paper with a knife. My inclination towards meticulous details, clean lines, and flat colors also suits paper cutting. I'm also an ink illustrator, a photographer, a designer, and a creative writer, but it was paper art that allowed me to go down my own unique path.

Could you share with us how you draw inspiration from nature and how you transform the inspiration into paper artworks?

The patterns in nature are one of my inspirations. These organic patterns can be distinguished by color, line, shape, and texture. When certain patterns jump out at me, I take a photo, or get a vision of a composition, and jot down notes on my sketchbook. You can find these patterns in places as tiny as the intricate lace of a decaying leaf, or as large as the layered hills and clouds of a rolling landscape. I then channel them into my art, whether through the designs that I draw from my imagination, or the color combinations I use, or the textures I build with my layers.

How did you find your style in paperwork? What is the most distinguishing feature of your work in your opinion?

In fact, I hadn't discovered traditional paper cutting until years after I pursued this form of art. Thus, I was given creative freedom in my mind to develop my work without being influenced by other artists or comparing my art with theirs. This clean slate allowed me to cultivate my methods in my own way, which led to unexpected visual results. Although the use of color, clean lines, and delicate cuts are all distinguishing features of my work, I would say that the multi-layered approach is my most distinct stylistic trait.

How do you stay passionate about paper art? Has there ever been a moment when you felt that you would like to take a break?

Only once in the past six years have I wanted a break from paper art. At that time, I had been pushing myself to cut more intricately with thinner lines and was burned out on overly complicated designs. To find a new direction, I took a few weeks off and did illustration and photography instead. Somewhere along the line, a new focus surfaced: depth and color. That was when I began my abstract landscapes series, where my palettes became more elaborate, and I started working with 30, 40, or more than 50 layers. After this reboot, my passion for paper art flourished again.

Do you have any advice or suggestions to those just starting out in paper art?

I always tell people to do what comes naturally to them. Although good techniques and materials can be shared, creative vision cannot. Let your inspirations fuel ideas, but build that fueled vehicle to your ideal specification. When you do things in your own way, it will be easier than trying to follow someone else's rules. Turn anything that you think is a mistake into something new and keep going because every "mistake" can lead to an innovation that sets your work apart.

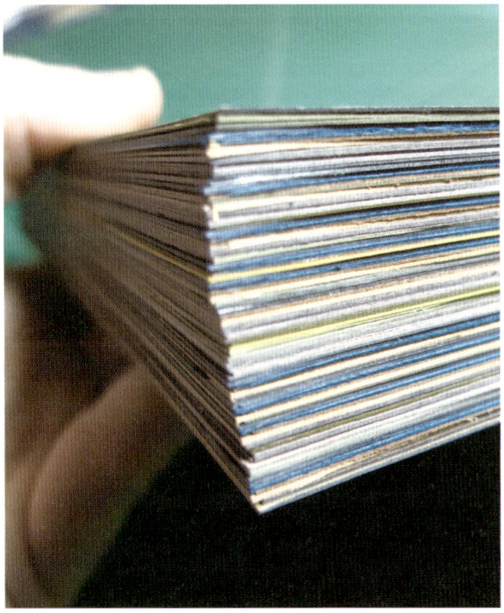

Where the Sky Fell

Cenotes and tree root caves seem to form magical portals, hidden throughout the overgrown landscape. In Hazel's sculptural version she employed 81 layers of paper plus spacers to give it a depth that viewers could imagine escaping down into.

Tools: *Craft knife, rivets*
Techniques: *Drawing, cutting, layering, riveting*

A Gift for Our Sea from the Sky

This two-centimeter sailing ship is caught in a squall among 49 layers of hand-cut paper. Though mostly roiling blue waves and dark clouds, the bit of metallic gold in the back shows hope for those who can weather the storm.

Tools: *Craft knife, archival glue*
Techniques: *Drawing, cutting, layering, gluing*

Echoes after the Flood

Hazel sketched out the idea for this work after hiking several slot canyons in the desert.

Tools: *Craft knife, archival glue*
Techniques: *Drawing, cutting, layering, gluing*

▲ Whirlpool

With 28 layers of hand-cut paper, the work is a stylized illustration to depict the concept of movement.

Tools: *Craft knife, archival glue*
Techniques: *Drawing, cutting, layering, gluing*

▸ The Rabbit Hole

With 30 layers of hand-cut paper, it was inspired by filigree and other decorative arts.

Tools: *Craft knife, archival glue*
Techniques: *Drawing, cutting, layering, gluing*

We Keep Walking to Where the Days End

Each day brings new adventures and wondrous possibilities. But likewise, by charging down the fascinating paths of our lives, each step brings us closer to our final days. This artwork reflects upon our mortality, and how the fact that everything ends is what makes life even more beautiful.

Tools: *Craft knife, archival glue*
Techniques: *Drawing, cutting, layering, gluing*

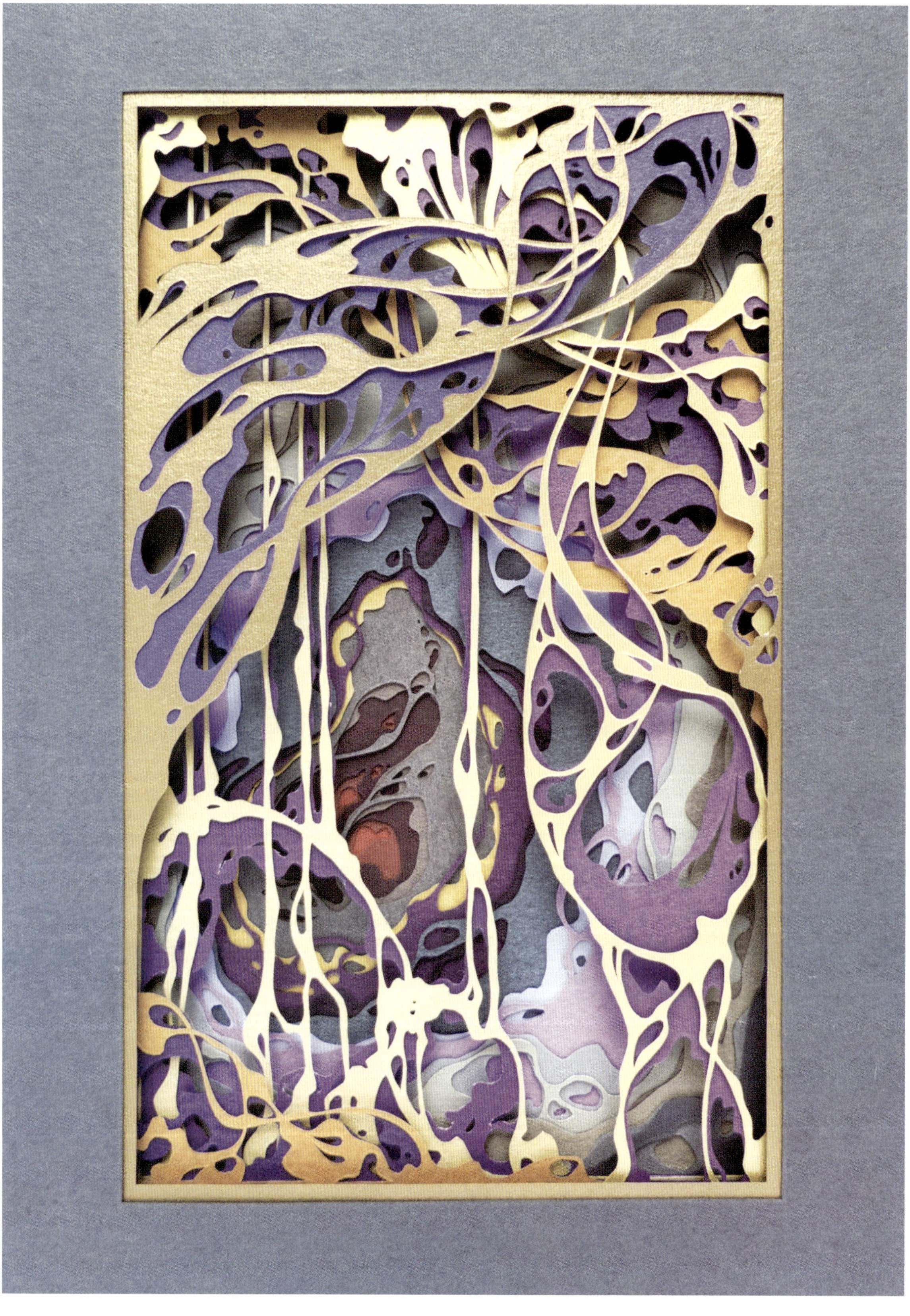

◂ **Caught in Your Chrysalis, We Grow**

This paper artwork is made of 26 layers of hand-cut paper. Spacers were used between the layers to create added depth.

Tools: *Craft knife, archival glue*
Techniques: *Drawing, cutting, layering, gluing*

▴ **Leaves Fall**

Hazel applied a mix of symmetrical ornamental design with stylized natural elements to make this seven-layer paper cutting work.

Tools: *Craft knife, archival glue*
Techniques: *Drawing, cutting, layering, gluing*

Héloïse Bossard

"The natural world offers me an endless source of inspiration."

Under the name of Au Détour du Papier, **Héloïse Bossard** creates paper cutting art inspired by elements of the natural world—mainly flowers and animals along with patterns and shapes found in nature. Always keen to explore new techniques, she is using cyanotype (a photographic printing process utilizing sunshine) to produce Prussian blueprints of her original paper cuttings.

▲ Samara Seeds

Héloïse carried out a 30-day challenge in 2019, where she explored the textures and patterns that could be observed in nature. "Samara Seeds," also known as "helicopter seeds," is one of the pieces made during that period.

Tool: *Scalpel knife with #11 blade*
Technique: *Cutting*

▸ Ginkgo Forest Growing on the Palm of My Hand

This artwork pays tribute to Héloïse's grandmother who planted a ginkgo tree in her garden. The tree was planted as a reminder of passing on the idea of taking care of the natural world to the next generation. She hand-coated a piece of white paper with a light-sensitive liquid. Once the paper dried, she put the piece of artwork on it under the sun. After being washed, the exposed photogram turned a vibrant Prussian blue color.

Tool: *Scalpel knife with #11 blade*
Techniques: *Cutting, cyanotype*

Interview with **Héloïse Bossard**

When and how did you start your journey of paper art?

It started in 2017 when I was looking to change careers from architecture to graphic design. At that time, I had an opportunity to work with a French paper artist. This experience made me realize how much I missed working directly with materials, especially paper.

Could you briefly describe your process of creating a paper artwork?

Once I have an idea of what subject I desire to work on, I will do image research to understand the subject better and draw sketches from the pictures. To create a single sheet of paper artwork, I transfer my drawing on the back of the paper and start cutting carefully. Cutting a lot of details allows me to be highly concentrated and transform this moment into a meditative experience.

Why is paper art special to you compared with other forms of art?

Ordinary as it is, paper offers infinite possibilities and can be turned into something extraordinary or used in an unexpected way. Although most of my artworks are two-dimensional, I find the versatility of paper very interesting and enjoy discovering how other paper artists play with it.

How did you find your style of paper art? What is the most distinguishing feature of your work?

I love exploring new techniques and like to see my style keep changing. In the beginning, I made colorful paper illustrations using a multi-layered technique while in recent years I mostly create single-layered artworks. Constantly, people say that they can see some Japanese inspiration in my work. That might result from my experience of living in Tokyo for two years. I probably unconsciously add some Japanese elements to my work. If I could define my paper cutting today, I would say that it's delicate and poetic, fine, gracious, meticulous, and well-thought-out.

Many pieces of your artwork involve animals and plants. What is it that you find so attractive about the natural world?

The natural world offers me an endless source of inspiration. There are countless animal and plant species in nature, and there are nuances even within each type of them. Take the ginkgo as an example, if you were to compare a hundred leaves, you would realize each one of them is different from the others. Isn't it fascinating?

How did you come up with the creative idea of combining cyanotype and paper cutting?

An original paper cutting artwork can be pricey, and not everyone can afford to buy one to hang at home. As I believe art shouldn't be reserved only for an elite, I look for ways to reproduce some of my paper cuttings at an affordable price. Also, I'm attached to the idea that each artwork is unique, so I tried to find a technique that would create subtle differences from one print to another during reproduction. First I tried linocut inks to imprint my layered paper artwork but was not satisfied with the result. Then I came across this cyanotype technique, which consists of using a photosensitive product to "print with the sun." Although it's mostly used with plants or photographic negatives, I decided to try that process with a single-sheet paper cutting piece. It worked so well! Since the hand coating and object placement slightly differ from one copy to another, each print is unique.

What is the biggest challenge you have experienced in your career as a paper artist so far? How did you overcome it?

One of my biggest challenges is to overcome the fear of a blank page. When I haven't decided what to do next, I feel excited to try every possibility but also feel scared when I don't know where I'm heading. The start of 2019 was hard for me as I was overwhelmed by too many questions regarding my art and doubted myself frequently. I couldn't draw anything, let alone cut. After some months of confusion, I set myself a goal to create one paper cutting piece per day for 30 days. With a goal, a theme, and a format, I gradually freed myself from the blockage.

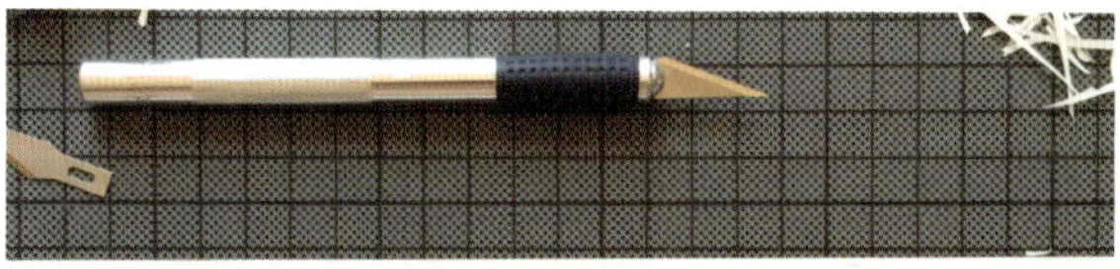

La Vague

"La Vague" (The Wave) is inspired by *The Great Wave off Kanagawa* painted by Katsushika Hokusai. To emphasize the movements of the waves, Héloïse adjusted the curve and position of some lines while cutting.

Tool: *Scalpel knife with #11 blade*
Technique: *Cutting*

The Call of the Mermaid

When sketching this project, Héloïse was just playing with lines and geometrical forms without a specific idea in mind. At some point, the diamonds, lines, and circles started to look like a mermaid tailfin. She then decided to emphasize this vision by adding a face profile.

Tool: *Scalpel knife with #11 blade*
Technique: *Cutting*

Pippa Dyrlaga

"I prefer a more intuitive approach, so my work can be reflective of my experiences or feelings at that particular time."

Pippa Dyrlaga is a paper cutting artist and printmaker based in Yorkshire, England. She uses traditional techniques to create contemporary artworks inspired by the natural world and the things around her. The simplicity of a blank sheet of paper appeals to her because it has so many possibilities to be turned into something beautiful or meaningful.

This Fragile World

This piece was created for the ABV Gallery show "Paper Trails" in Atlanta, Georgia, USA, in 2019. Abstract forms and organic patterns grow from tears in the paper, creating strange landscapes.

Tools: *Knife, 36 gsm washi paper, acrylic paint*
Techniques: *Cutting, painting*

Interview with **Pippa Dyrlaga**

When and how did you start your journey of paper art?

I have been using paper as a medium since around 2009 when I was a postgraduate student. It was an unintentional discovery, a progression from drawing and cutting them out, which resonated with me much clearer and stronger than any other methods of creating art. As an art student, I had enough time and courage to experiment with paper and look at the context of paper art in both history and the contemporary art scene. Those experiments and research were very inspirational and increased my love of the medium and drove me to continue working this way.

Could you briefly describe your process of creating a piece of paper artwork? Which part do you enjoy the most?

Generally, I start with a vague idea or a starting point in mind instead of a full plan. Sometimes I will make smaller test pieces to see if certain patterns or cuts will work. I work in sections and add detail as I go along, allowing the composition of my pieces to change flexibly. With the pencil drawing on the reverse side of the paper, I flip it over and start cutting.

I enjoy the whole process of making the pieces because it is meditative and calming. The challenge of paper cutting is a very personal journey since each piece has its own victories and trials. I can share the finished pieces with everyone, but the process of creating is an exclusive experience.

Why do you prefer paper art?

I think every artist has a medium that speaks to them and helps them express themselves the best. For me, the medium is paper cutting. Although I had a strong desire for creativity after graduating from university, it took me a few years to explore the form of art that would be most suitable for me. Once I had discovered paper cutting, it was like a light bulb moment.

How do you turn the inspirations and ideas in your head into actual paper works?

I draw a lot of inspiration from nature, architecture, design, and pop culture. I grew up living on a canal boat in beautiful countryside, so the surrounding riverbanks and typical English countryside views inspire me a lot. When visualizing the inspirations and ideas, I prefer a more intuitive approach, so my work can be reflective of my experiences or feelings at that particular time.

Have you ever experienced any creative block? How did you overcome it?

Of course. Focusing on the creative block made it even worse, so the best way for me to deal with it was to just keep working on as slowly as I needed to without pressuring myself to create something complete. Every time a creative block occurs, I will work on a pattern or re-create something I have already made by increasing details, changing the context, or setting myself a simple brief to make it better.

Animals and plants can be seen in many of your works. Why do they fascinate you?

I feel very drawn to the elegance in the natural world. A theory by Edward O. Wilson, called the biophilia hypothesis, suggests that humans have an innate need to seek out and connect with nature and other forms of life, which resonates strongly with me.

Are there any artists that you appreciate, in the field of paper art or other forms of art? What have you learned from them?

There are two paper artists particularly inspiring to me. Bovey Lee was a paper artist whom I discovered when I first started cutting paper. Her work was, and still is, completely mind-blowing. It shows that art is not only beautiful and painstakingly handcrafted but also meaningful and can convey a strong message. Another master craftswoman is Woodlucker, whose dedication to detail and the passion for her beautiful work can be seen in every piece she makes.

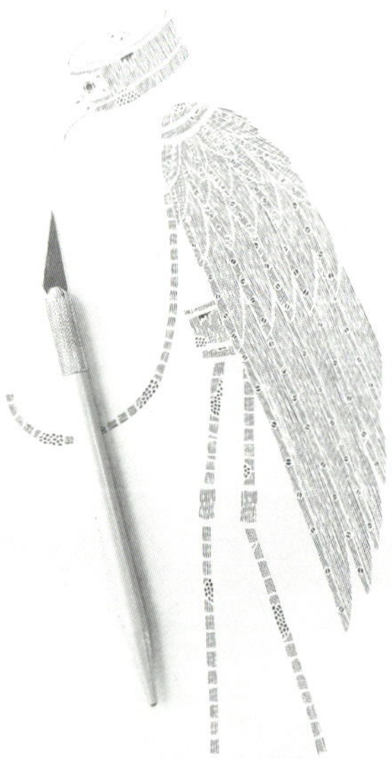

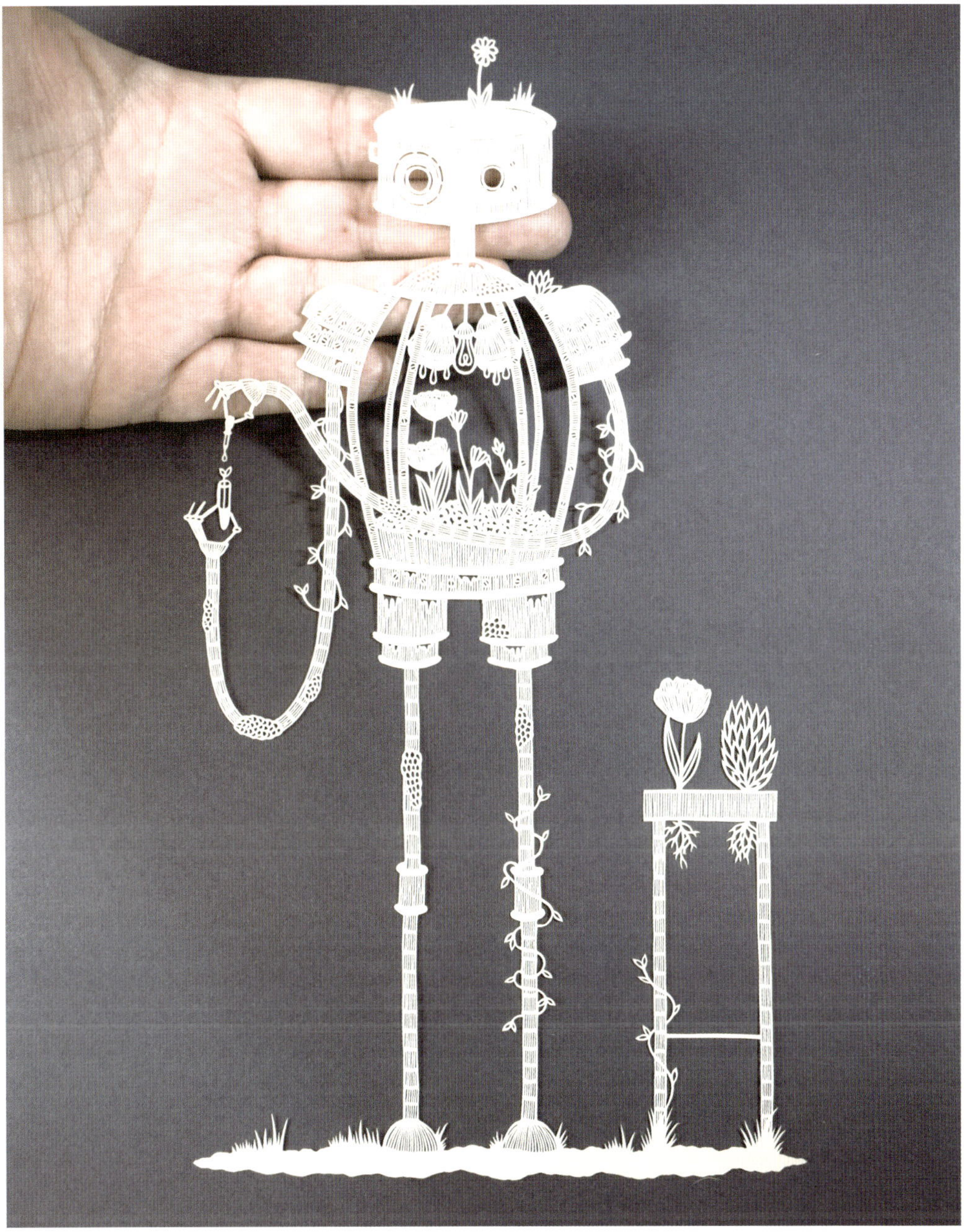

The Ornithologist, The Botanist

These two pieces are part of a series of obsolete robots whose sole purpose is to understand the natural world around them, in a world where humans are no longer here. These man-made machines approach the world with respect and wonder of something that isn't of themselves. Sized 6 in × 10.5 in, these artworks were shown in the Salon des Beaux-Arts, Paris, in 2018.

Tools: *Knife, 36 gsm washi paper*
Technique: *Cutting*

▲ **Foraging in the Tree Tops**

This piece depicts an autumn scene of squirrels preparing for winter.

Tools: *Knife, 135 gsm paper*
Technique: *Cutting*

▸ **Sweetpea & Tendrils**

Through this piece of artwork, Pippa attempted to capture the delicacy of Sweetpea flowers.

Tools: *Knife, 36 gsm washi paper*
Technique: *Cutting*

Sinking

This piece was made around the time when Pippa's grandfather passed away. Through "Sinking," she wanted to capture the loss of something beautiful.

Tools: *Knife, 46 gsm washi paper*
Technique: *Cutting*

Riverside II

This piece invoked the life around the banks of the English rivers that Pippa grew up on.

Tools: *Knife, 135 gsm paper*
Technique: *Cutting*

By the River

This piece was also about the life around the banks, but Pippa employed different and lighter paper for it.

Tools: *Knife, 36 gsm washi paper*
Technique: *Cutting*

Every Night, She Would Conjure an Entire Forest in Her Dreams

It was inspired by the dreams that Pippa was having at that time. She has always taken a lot of inspiration from her dreams because the symbolism of dreams is very fascinating to her.

Tools: *Knife, paints*
Techniques: *Cutting, painting*

Matriarch: Gaia

This piece was inspired by the power, knowledge, and life experience of women living through the 20th century.

Tools: *Knife, washi paper, acrylic paint*
Techniques: *Cutting, gluing, painting*

Marina Adamova

"Handmade art, especially paper art, remains unique in this highly-digitalized world."

Marina Adamova is a self-taught paper artist who likes difficulties. Feeling constant self-development necessary, she enjoys exploring new ways of visual expression in her works and is specifically interested in combining illustrative and paper cutting approaches. Also, as a graphic designer, she is fond of experimenting with lettering compositions.

Елина

Christmas 2019

The white scenery piece was made as an illustration for a print program to announce the Christmas activities for Mont-Royal Avenue in the neighborhood of Plateau-Mont-Royal in Montreal, Canada.

Tools: *Olfa art knife, white glue, Pergraphica white 300 gsm paper, Canson glossy gold paper*
Techniques: *Cutting, gluing, folding*

Interview with **Marina Adamova**

When and how did you start your journey of paper art?

I started on my way in 2013 when I held my first personal exhibition as an illustrator with black-and-white graphics called "Old Winter's Fairytales." As it was launched in May, I was asked to add some colors and flowers to the black-and-white concept with paper art techniques to the artwork by the exhibition curator. Then I decided to make paper illustrations for different fairy tales, that's how my first paper series for *Alice in Wonderland* came to life.

Why do you prefer paper art rather than other forms?

Paper is my love. I enjoy working with it every minute because of its texture and the visual result. In terms of volume and shadows, it is really impressive and can fully draw viewers' attention. Besides, paper art is a personal narrative to me as the viewer can feel the warmth and energy of the creator's hands even from its digital copy through the computer monitor. Handmade art, especially paper art, remains unique in this highly-digitalized world.

You have done a lot of commissioned projects as well as personal artworks. What are the differences between the two kinds of projects?

For personal projects, sometimes they are really difficult since I'm the one to motivate myself, to manage the process, and to criticize the result. At the same time, however, I'm free to make everything that comes to my mind, which is a great time for me. Yet, I also enjoy commissioned projects as they give me the chance to expand my horizons. In addition, it drives me to improve my ability in terms of communication and efficiency because I need to follow the brief of the project in limited time. Sometimes, I have to even develop new techniques to meet the client's expectations. Therefore, it's very challenging but rewarding as it gives me the right kick for further development.

You seem to enjoy traveling very much. What kind of influence does your wanderlust have on your artworks?

Yes, I'm fond of traveling very much. It's like a fresh gulp of air to me and gives me personal experience that I can use to create my art. It makes me stay inspired for a long time even after the journey and keeps me in a positive mood, which is the best condition for creation.

How did you find your style on paper art? What do you think is the most distinguishing feature of your work?

I started using colored paper in my works but, little by little, I realized that I prefer to use white paper for my pieces, with one or two colors for some details in the composition. Besides, my style is affected by the 300 gsm paper I use, of which the thickness and weight maintain the visual of two-dimension in some of my artworks even though I employ more of a three-dimensional approach.

Is there anything that you hope to improve? How do you plan to improve it?

There're different techniques of paper art existing today, and I always remain curious to try something new and to develop my own way of using it. Also, there're so many different papers on the market now, and I'll be happy to experiment with them, which might improve my skills unexpectedly.

Could you give some suggestions to newcomers?

Please keep your patience and stay calm. It can be tricky the first time, but then it'll give you a lot of joy and enlighten your way of thinking. For something practical, you would do best to try a few types of paper with different weights to find the one that fits you the best, control the amount of glue to avoid a dirty-looking result, and put your final artwork in the frame with glass to prolong the life of your efforts.

Autumn Opener

"Autumn Opener" is part of the "Almanac" project where Marina collaborated with 18 lettering and calligraphy artists from different countries. The project aims to show the unique beauty of each culture through writing and dialog about the differences at different times of a year in these countries, emphasizing that visual art is a special language uniting people beyond borders and time. For this piece, Magdalena Konečná created the composition which Marina embodied in paper, color, and volume.

Tools: *Olfa art knife, white glue, awl*
Techniques: *Cutting, gluing, folding*

PAC Christmas: 4 Calling Birds

As a member of Paper Artist Collective (PAC), Marina and other artists have been invited to take part in global collaborations from time to time. In this Christmas activity, Marina was allocated to illustrate the line "4 Calling Birds." She took "4" as the main element which formed a frame for the plot movement in the composition, expressing the idea of some tragic development inside the stability.

Tools: *Gmund papers, Olfa art knife, white glue, awl*
Techniques: *Cutting, gluing, folding*

PAC Alphabet: Z

This piece was for another PAC collaboration where each participant was allocated three colors and a letter from the English alphabet. Marina got Kielder Moss, Botanical Green, Brooklands Green, and the letter *Z*. She was inspired by the vocal association between *Z* and snoring. Besides, *Z* is the last letter in the alphabet, so the sleeping concept looked symbolic. Later, a mermaid image was determined to fit the chosen colors and follow the silhouette of *Z*.

Tools: *Papers of Kielder Moss 250 gsm, Botanical Green 250 gsm, and Brooklands Green 250 gsm, Olfa art knife, white glue, awl*
Techniques: *Cutting, gluing, folding*

Summer Opener

Collaborated with the lettering artist Eduardo Morgan Gaytán, Marina created this piece for her "Almanac" project.

Tools: *Olfa art knife, white glue, awl*
Techniques: *Cutting, gluing, folding*

Janvier

"Janvier," meaning January in French, is also a piece included in the "Almanac" project. The lettering composition was created by Svetlana Lissov, then Marina transformed it into paper art.

Tools: *Olfa art knife, white glue, awl*
Techniques: *Cutting, gluing, folding*

Sota

"I am creating artworks to express that nothing is single-sided and that everything must have two or more dimensions."

Sota is a self-taught paper cutting artist who emphasizes the appeal of black paper cutouts while using light, shadow, and colors. In addition to his production of art, he also performs improvised paper cutting and holds workshops to draw public attention to paper art.

Black Cat

The cat is one of the most common subjects in Sota's artworks. The cutout is black with bright yellow and vivid red in the background emphasizing the presence of a lovely cat and its curled tail.

Tools: *Knife, glue*
Techniques: *Cutting, gluing*

Interview with **Sota**

When and how did you start your journey with paper art? Why is paper art special to you?

I have always been fond of art, especially painting. One day in 2010, I discovered the art of paper cutting on TV. Finding it interesting, I started to do it myself. I prefer paper art for several reasons. First, I appreciate the contrast between black and white that paper cutting achieves. Also, by cutting paper, I am able to create sharp lines. Besides, paper is so versatile that paper art can be simultaneously two-dimensional and three-dimensional.

Could you briefly describe your process of creating a paper artwork? How do you choose your color palette?

Firstly, I determine the motif and look for references. While referring to the motif, I cut the sheets of black paper directly without any sketches. Later, I paste the color paper to the cutouts. Traditionally, Japanese paper cutting is black-and-white, and the black and white parts are sometimes separated. As for my artworks, I give more prominence to the black part while using the white to accentuate the black. My color palette is built on experimentation with various colors and what I have seen and noticed around me. When choosing the colors, what I consider the most is how I can emphasize the black cutouts and make them more compelling. Since the black cutouts are the main subjects of my paper cutting, the pieces of color paper pasted to them are sometimes irregular, which both maintains the texture of paper and gives my artworks a playful sense.

Where do you usually get inspiration? Have you ever experienced creative block? How did you overcome it?

My inspirations are often from nature, creatures, and things around me. Sometimes I get blocked, but once I am away from paper cutting and do something else, I will spontaneously want to try again soon.

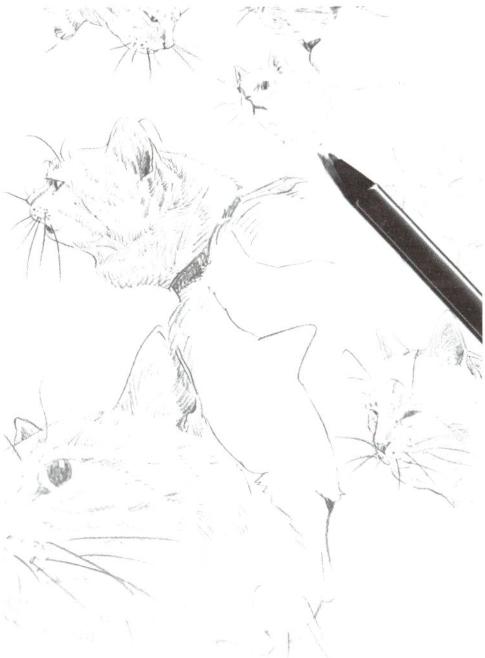

What are some common themes of your artworks? What do you want to express through them?

Although some of my artworks base the motifs on the forms, the overall concept of my creation is "表裏一体," a Japanese idiom indicating that the opposite sides actually define each other and are integrated into one. If there is the interior, there must also be the exterior; if there is light, there must also be shadows; if there is no death, there won't be life... This is my philosophy of life, and I want to convey this message through not only my work but also the creative process no matter what the theme is or which technique I apply. One example is that in my paper cutting, the black cutouts are actually accentuated by the uncut and cannot be seen without it. In short, I am creating artworks to express that nothing is single-sided and that everything must have two or more dimensions.

Have you experienced a singularly stunning and impressive piece of paper artwork? What did you learn from it?

The paper cutting of Takidaira Jiro, a Japanese master of paper art, amazes me very much. When I was watching his work, the delicate and warm atmosphere, as well as the gritty cut and bold composition of his work, made me realize how important being the one and only is.

Do you have any suggestions to those who just recently dove into paper art?

I think paper has infinite possibilities, so you can try various things freely without caring about what type of art it is. By all means—cutting, folding, pasting, and so on—you can create a work that you are satisfied with.

Choco

Choco is the pet dog of Sota's friend. This piece depicts the softness of its fur and, more importantly, its expression while looking gently at its owner.

Tools: *Knife, glue*
Techniques: *Cutting, gluing*

Girl, Man, Sneakers, Men's Sneakers, Man in Hat

These five pieces in pop colors are in Sota's fashion series. In both "Girl" and "Man," Sota gave prominence to the overall shapes of the characters instead of their facial expressions, allowing space for the viewers' imagination. In the two pieces about sneakers, Sota depicted the shoes and feet objectively and created a stylish atmosphere. Unlike classic paper cutting, "Man in Hat" outstands the black cutout by applying lots of colors.

Tools: *Knife, glue*
Techniques: *Cutting, gluing*

Amabie

This piece portrays the legendary Japanese mermaid-like god, Amabie, who is emerging from the sea. According to the legend, this god lives in the sea and will show up to protect people when there is a pandemic. In the background, the movements of the waves and the red round sun create a familiar Japanese feeling. Sota made this paper cutting during the COVID-19 period, hoping people around the world will stay healthy.

Tools: *Knife, glue*
Techniques: *Cutting, gluing*

Gujo Hachiman Castle

Gujo Hachiman Castle is a famous site in Sota's hometown, Gujo, Japan. This piece of artwork depicts the beautiful castle and the river flowing through the town under the full moon, conveying the tranquil but gorgeous atmosphere of the town.

Tools: *Knife, glue*
Techniques: *Cutting, gluing*

Ale Rambar

"For me, the function of art is to change society and to bring attention to problems in our daily lives."

Ale Rambar uses topographical techniques—usually applied in geography—to talk about issues of tolerance for the environment in which we live, for the people who live in it, and for our representations of love. It is an artistic exploration in favor of tolerance and equality, expressed in works of art that seek to open spaces for conversation. (Portrait photo by Domestika.)

Of Paper and Wind

In ancient China, dragons were depicted chasing flaming pearls symbolizing wisdom, power, prosperity, and immortality. Alluding to the dragons, "Chasing Pearls Collection" is an artistic representation of people, specifically queer persons, who are chasing their own pearls—ideals of knowledge and lifestyle. "Of Paper and Wind" is one of the pieces in the collection, specially sewed with feathers.

Tools: *Acid-free and PH-neutral paper and adhesives, feathers, watercolor*
Techniques: *Drawing, painting, cutting, gluing, assembling, sewing*

When and how did you start your journey with paper art?

When I was studying architecture in college, I had to make many topographic terrain models simply by hand, cutting cardboard, foam board, card stock, and various materials. For my thesis project, I joined a program called "Landscape Architecture." After analyzing kilometers of topographic maps, I began to imagine what would happen if I transformed human bodies into sculptures the same way as I transformed terrains into architectonic models. These experiences evolved into my artistic work, which is based on the topographic analysis of the human form through three-dimensional compositions made with layers of paper.

Could you briefly describe your process of creating a paper artwork?

I prefer to create my pieces in collections, so first I envision the concept behind the collection and the images that could portray that idea. After that, I imagine, draw, and sketch my art pieces as freely as I can, going wild with ideas. Then, I draw all of the layers, cut, glue, and assemble them. It's not a piece-by-piece process since I usually finish all the pieces of a collection almost at the same time.

Apart from paper, you sometimes apply different materials, such as pearls and feathers, to your creation. How did you come up with the creative idea of using them?

I have been trying various materials to keep my creative juices flowing. At this moment, I see paper as the base of my art and experiment on top of it. In my last collection, I sewed in pearls and feathers to bring a new element to my compositions. Sometimes I stumble into these materials and keep them in mind until they find their way into my art pieces. They may come from anywhere, and I just keep my eyes open for future opportunities.

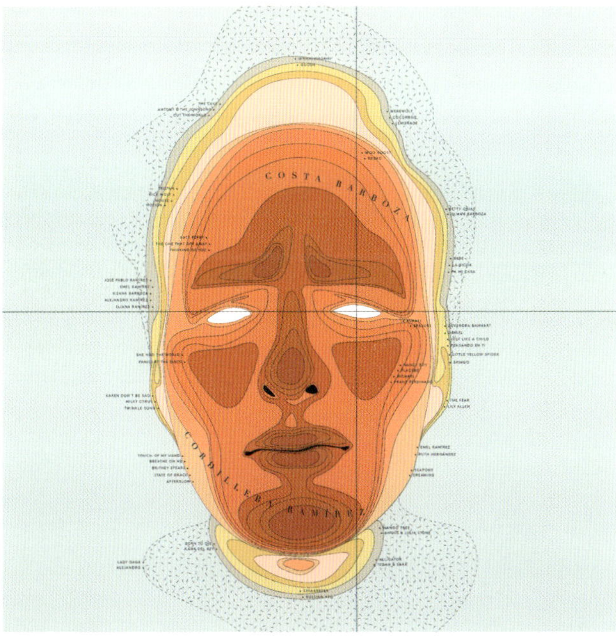

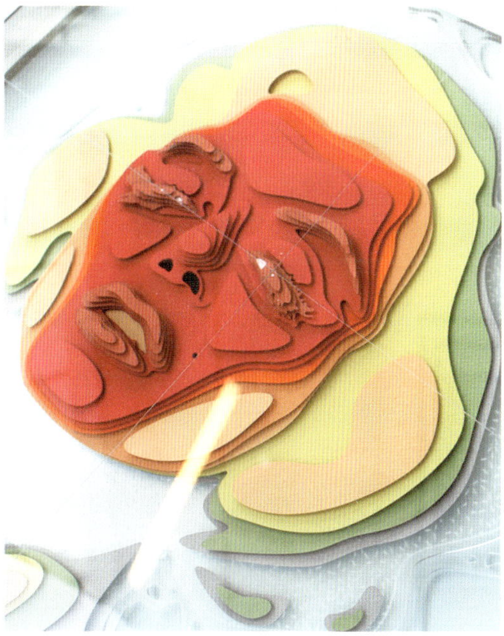

Where do you find inspiration?

I usually base my pieces on real-life stories that come from my community. For me, the function of art is to change society and to bring attention to problems in our daily lives. I use my art to open conversations about the experiences of all kinds of people in regards to their sexual identity, or the discrimination they have felt due to it. This is something that I consider necessary for our society to advance together.

Your work has been displayed in a few exhibitions. What is the biggest challenge of preparing for exhibitions compared with creating new pieces in your studio?

There are completely different processes. When I'm at my studio, I only need to focus on creating art at my own pace. While planning an exhibition, I have to put on my marketing hat and complement it with museography and event design. The days and hours before an exhibition are hectic—everything has to come together as you have envisioned it, and you should be there to present it.

Although art and design is increasingly aided by computer software, handcraft continues to fascinate people. What qualities of paper art make it so powerful and timeless?

My favorite quality of paper art is that paper is everywhere. We unconsciously choose to give it importance or not, considering it a creative outlet or just letting it pass. This is also a metaphor that I carried into my creative process—many issues regarding tolerance are like paper that we are in contact with every day, and some of us ignore them while some do something about them.

Would you mind sharing your suggestions for those who are just starting to dive into paper art?

First of all, be patient, because paper art involves a lot of practice, and we learn it through trial and error. Second, learn about the materials and tools since not all papers will stand the test of time and not all adhesives will work well. Third, experiment as much as you possibly can and always step out of your comfort zone to research new concepts.

3 a.m.

This piece is a part of a micro collection of three pieces, representing portraits of people Ale met during his first trip to China. "3 a.m." is a portrait of a man Ale got to meet at 3 a.m. in Beijing, with a small piece of dichroic film added.

Tools: *Acid-free and PH-neutral paper and adhesives, watercolor, dichroic film*
Techniques: *Drawing, painting, cutting, gluing, assembling*

Compact

"Compact" is one of the pieces in "Chasing Pearls Collection" sewed with pearls. This piece represents the sensation Ale felt while transiting through the public system in China—compact, tight, and still with lots of movement.

Tools: *Acid-free and PH-neutral paper and adhesives, pearls*
Techniques: *Drawing, painting, cutting, gluing, assembling, sewing*

Chao

Sewed with pearls, "Chao" is one of the pieces included in "Chasing Pearls Collection." In this collection, pearls are sewed in grid compositions to symbolize windows of openings, and the paper figures interact with these openings as if they were passages. Made on the last day during Ale's trip to China, "Chao" represents a farewell, while still looking back to the experience.

Tools: *Acid-free and PH-neutral paper and adhesives, pearls*
Techniques: *Drawing, painting, cutting, gluing, assembling, sewing*

▲ Discovery

"Discovery" is a piece in Ale's "Tolerance Collection" which addresses social issues that are close to his personal life. "I pass this voice to human beings, seeking to exemplify observations of our upbringing as Costa Ricans on issues of gender, sexism, and sexual diversity towards what I find important to draw attention. Just like nature should be respected, many people also deserve respect in the fight for equality," said Ale.

Tools: *Acid-free and PH-neutral paper and adhesives*
Techniques: *Drawing, painting, cutting, gluing, assembling*

▸ I Don't Want to Wear My Hair Long

This piece was created after Ale asked, "What is something you couldn't do as a child just because you were born male or female?" For girls, it was making anything with their hair other than wearing it as their parents told them. This piece is included in Ale's "Tolerance Collection."

Tools: *Acid-free and PH-neutral paper and adhesives*
Techniques: *Drawing, painting, cutting, gluing, assembling*

Torn

This art piece is the final product of an audiovisual project collaborated with the producer Pablo Serrano. The audiovisual production of "Torn" presents the deconstruction of a canonically attractive masculine figure, as a critique of stereotypical beauty and fragile masculinity.

Tools: *Acid-free and PH-neutral paper and adhesives, watercolor*
Techniques: *Drawing, painting, cutting, gluing, assembling, tearing*

The Award for Gender Equity of the European Union in Costa Rica

Ale had the honor to design the award which is delivered annually to a different association for their continued effort to search for equality and protect people at social risk.

Tools: *Acid-free and PH-neutral paper and adhesives, gold leaf*
Techniques: *Drawing, painting, cutting, gluing, assembling*

Owen Gildersleeve

"Paper is the medium that I feel most comfortable expressing myself with because it's very hands-on and gives me lots of freedom and flexibility."

Owen Gildersleeve is an award-winning artist specializing in handcrafted illustration, set design, and art direction. His unique style, honed over the past ten years, brings graphic designs to life through carefully hand-cut layers and playful use of light and shadow. His practice ranges from intricate paper illustrations and animations to large-scale sets, window displays, and installations.

CAST
AWAY

San Francisco

Owen was commissioned to create this cover illustration for *San Francisco Magazine* to accompany their annual ranking of all 101 Bay Area cities. The illustration brings together the iconic towers from the four Bay Area districts to create a seamless paper cut landscape.

Tools: *Scalpel, foam board*
Techniques: *Cutting, assembling*

Interview with **Owen Gildersleeve**

When and how did you start your journey of paper art?

I've always been interested in fine art, especially "tactile artists" like Robert Rauschenberg, Anselm Kiefer, and Cy Twombly who use a lot of different techniques and materials in their work. When I went to study graphic design, I was immediately drawn to designers like Stefan Sagmeister and Alan Fletcher who apply lots of hands-on processes in their work. Then over time, I started to find materials and techniques that gave me more flexibility than others. This is how I came to working with paper, a very versatile and affordable medium, available in a nice range of colors and easy to transfer my designs onto.

Could you briefly describe your process of creating a paper artwork?

I begin each project with rough pencil sketches, getting down the initial ideas and concepts. Later, I draw up the design digitally in Adobe Illustrator, refining the forms and working out the color palette. After that, I use the digital drawing as a template, printing out the linework on sheets of color paper—but backward so that once it's cut out, I can flip over the page and conceal the lines. Having done the cutting, I assemble the artwork using pieces of card and foam core to create the depth between the layers. I often photograph the final artwork myself in my studio, using natural light that helps to give nice soft shadows and retains the paper textures. Once everything is photographed, I will retouch and clean-up the image in Adobe Photoshop ready for final delivery.

Why is paper art special to you compared with other forms of art?

It's the medium that I feel most comfortable expressing myself with because it's very hands-on and gives me lots of freedom and flexibility. The final artworks can also look quite crisp and graphic, or more hands-on and craft-like depending on the paper stocks and finish to choose. I've recently been enjoying playing with the juxtaposition of chaotic free-flowing forms framed by a crisp cutout graphic layer that's quite effective.

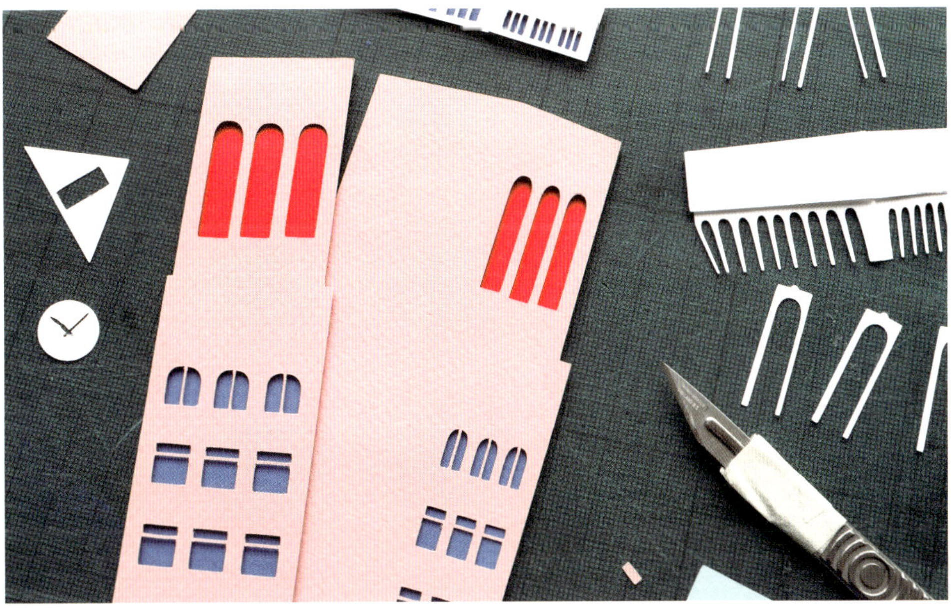

Where do you typically find inspiration?

For inspiration, I like to look outside of my design bubble because my best ideas come up when I'm on a walk, cycling, playing the drums, or at a gig—when I'm away from the screen and have a chance for my thoughts to settle. I read once that social media is the death of creativity, as people no longer give themselves the downtime needed for ideas to form. That really resonated with me, so even though it's hard to step away from the screen I try to go elsewhere for my inspiration as much as I can, especially when I'm getting into a creative block.

You have created many successful commissioned projects, especially covers for magazines. Could you share the key to impressing your clients and the viewers?

The main thing is just to be friendly and professional—that always goes a long way. In terms of the actual work, I do a lot of research around a subject, thinking about how best to approach an artwork, and why I've made certain creative decisions, such as form and color. Having that reasoning behind the choices I feel helps to ground the piece, and should hopefully help to lead to an artwork with an interesting take that feels fresh and engaging.

Although the use of computer software continues to creep further and further into art and design, handcrafted work still enthralls people. What do you think are the qualities of paper art that makes it timeless and powerful?

Paper art has been around for centuries, originally beginning as a decorative art form for celebrations in countries such as China. Having such a long history, it's something that people will always come back to. Also, everyone uses paper in their lives—whether it's to print onto, read or to create artworks—so people can relate to it as a medium. There's also a nice softness given by the grain and textures, which helps to add a human quality to the final artworks which people can connect with.

Lover, You Should've Come Over

This piece is the cover artwork for a special pressing of Jeff Buckley's track "Lover, You Should've Come Over" for the *Secret 7"* exhibition. It was sold during the show, with all proceeds going to the mental health charity Mind.

Tools: *Scalpel, foam board*
Techniques: *Cutting, assembling*

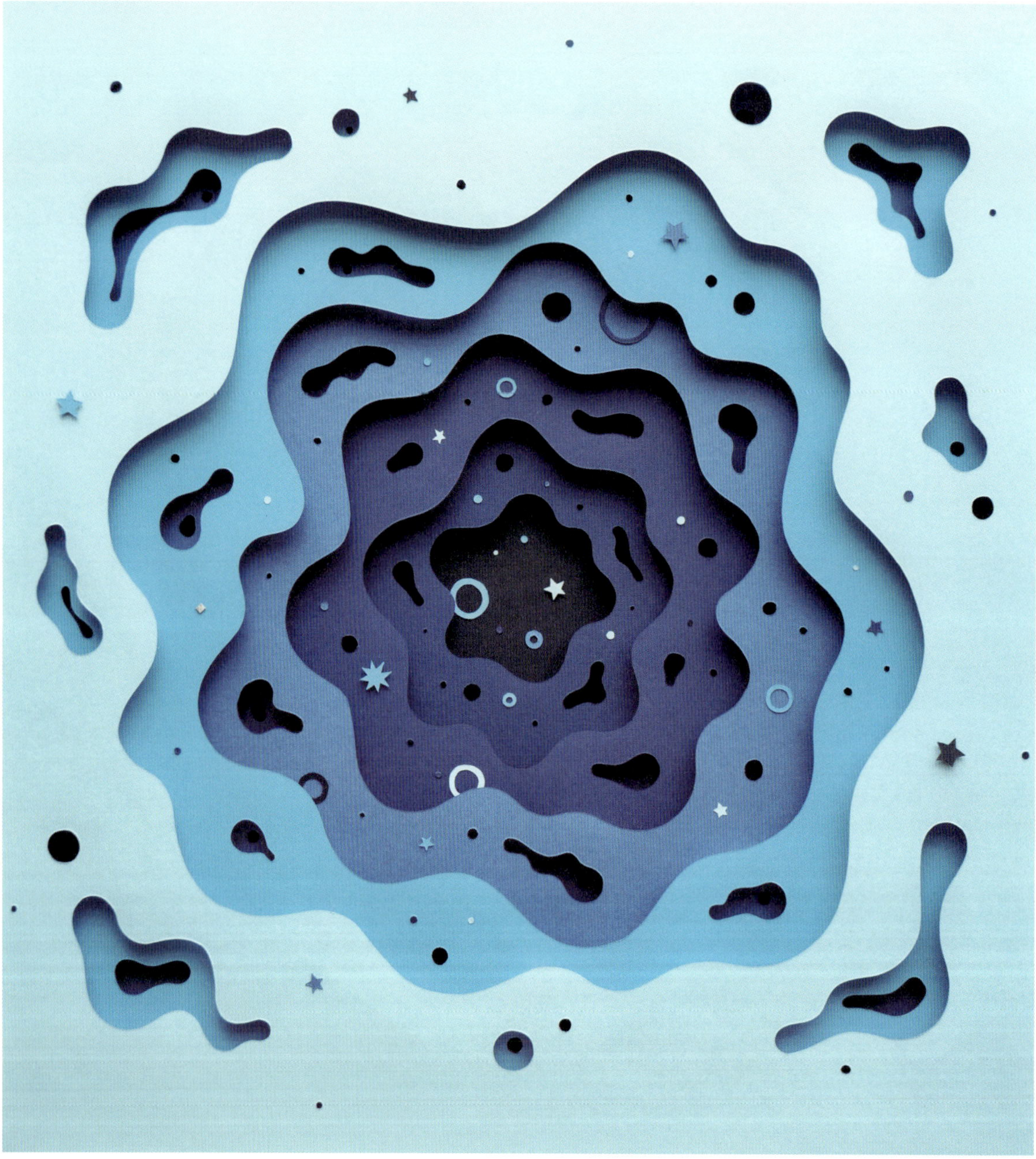

Distant Aeons

It is the first of a pair of personal illustrations exploring wormholes and parallel universes. The artworks were originally created for Owen's Paper Cut Exhibition, held to launch his first book.

Tools: *Scalpel, foam board*
Techniques: *Cutting, assembling*

SOL

SOL was designed as a celebration of the start of summer, through 12 circular forms that explore the powerful heat and energy of the sun. Partnered with G. F Smith's papers, Owen picked out a warm gradient of tones for the design. The final paper cuttings were layered up and photographed under natural daylight, fitting with the theme.

Tools: *Adobe Illustrator, Photoshop, scalpel, foam board, white tack*
Techniques: *Cutting, assembling, photographing*

▲ A Winter's Feast

Owen was commissioned by *Cook Magazine* to create the cover for their Christmas issue. Echoing the magazine's exploration of culture through food, he created an ensemble of traditional Italian dishes, Christmas decorations and festive imagery from intricately cut paper elements that reflect the warmth and indulgence of a traditional Italian Christmas.

Tools: *Adobe Illustrator, Photoshop, scalpel, foam board, white tack*
Techniques: *Cutting, assembling, photographing*

▸ Observations from the Unknown

For Owen's first US solo show, he created a body of nine original artworks informed by groundbreaking celestial data gathered by NASA's Kepler Spacecraft over the past nine years. These seemingly abstract pieces tell the tale of newly discovered exoplanets, visualizing nine of Kepler's greatest findings.

Tools: *Adobe Illustrator, scalpel, foam board*
Techniques: *Cutting, assembling*

Tania Lissova

"I want to bring happiness and pleasure to my viewers so my paper flowers are always in bloom and the plants never wither no matter what the weather is like outside."

Based in Russia, **Tania Lissova** is a paper artist who has been creating paper art for four years. Since the botanical theme is her favorite, most of her work revolves around paper plants and flowers, as well as cozy green corners.

ART
PLANTS
ARCHITECTURE

Botanical Collages

Inspired by various cozy corners in some plant lovers' houses, Tania has been making botanical corners in the form of collage for a few years now. All the collages are different—oriental style, red brick loft, rural house with wooden panels, brick house terrace—but they are united by her love of plants.

Tools: *Art knife, scissors, cutting mat, paper*
Techniques: *Cutting, gluing*

Interview with **Tania Lissova**

When and how did you start your journey of paper art?

When I was studying architecture and art at university in 2016, I created models of buildings and landscapes and drew illustrations as well. Although I became familiar with paper models, paper art remained unfamiliar to me. Later, out of curiosity, I studied paper art and learned from paper artists myself. I was interested in botany and wanted some plants for decoration to make my home cozier. However, the house plants I tried to grow never survived, so I came up with the idea of making flowers out of paper.

Could you briefly describe your process of creating a paper artwork? Which part do you enjoy the most?

I start by sketching what I want to do. Take a boutique as an example, I think over the color scheme and selection of flowers by sketching. After choosing paper based on color and texture, I transfer the drawings in parts onto colored paper, cut them out, and glue them together part by part. In the end, I pick up a plant or bouquet together to see the rest. Perhaps this is my favorite moment when everything has turned out as expected, or even better.

Why is paper art special to you compared with other forms of art?

In general, I always feel a craving for art and have tried different forms. Now there are an incredible amount of opportunities for creativity, among which paper art captivates me the most with its unusualness. The tools also seem to bring me a special experience. When I am using an art knife to cut out the details of plants, it feels like I'm drawing by carving freely—I have not experienced anything like it before.

Most of your artworks revolve around flowers and plants. Why are you so fascinated by them?

I love nature, and green is my favorite color. More importantly, the variety of flowers and plants is staggering. They are all unique without any detail repeated. Each leaf has its own vein pattern, and each flower has its own shape and color—plants seem to be an inexhaustible source of inspiration. Therefore, when I start to create a new paper plant, I always feel attracted and excited.

Your artworks have the magical power of putting viewers in a good mood! How do you evoke this experience?

Plants generally bring joy—fresh flowers, green house plants, gardens, flower fields, and forests create a feeling of harmony and vitality. I want to bring happiness and pleasure to my viewers so my paper flowers are always in bloom and the plants never wither no matter what the weather is like outside. Besides, I try to choose natural colors to resemble spring when everything comes to life, or summer when everything is blooming.

Could you share one of your favorite paper artists with us? What did you learn from him/her?

A few years ago, I learned about an English artist of the 18th century, Mary Granville Delany. She created a unique collection of paper plants using the paper mosaic technique. Without preliminary drawing, she immediately cut out the smallest details and glued them. Although I have never seen them in person, I have watched the photos of the work many times and always feel amazed at her accuracy. Besides, she came up with her own techniques instead of relying on those already known. It reminds me that we need to go our own way, do what we like rather than following the crowd.

Do you have any suggestions to those who just dove into paper art?

Firstly, find inspiration from everything around you—paintings, books, photographs, films, and nature. Then, try different paper art techniques, types of paper, tools, and sizes until you find the most suitable ones. Don't be upset if you can't do it right away because paper art takes time and effort. Most importantly, practice as often as possible to master the instrument. At the beginning of my journey, my fingers ached constantly, but that was worthwhile.

Wildflowers

This series of paper wildflowers was inspired by summer colors and flowers. From preparation to production, Tania spent a month to finish the flowers, and each of the flowers took about two hours to make.

Tools: *Art knife, scissors, cutting mat, paper, watercolor*
Techniques: *Painting, cutting, gluing*

Exotic Trio

Tania always creates trios composed of various plants. Those plants are always fresh and green even without water and care, as Tania envisioned. "Exotic Trio" is a typical example.

Tools: *Art knife, scissors, cutting mat, paper, watercolor*
Techniques: *Painting, cutting, gluing*

Sarah Suplina

"Art is about individuality and is an inner voice that helps to express one's self."

Sarah Suplina is a paper artist creating unique collages and snippets capturing the beauty of life. Her artworks have been exhibited all around the New York metro area, and in 2019, she opened her own studio. In addition to being a paper artist, she is an art teacher in New Rochelle, New York. (Portrait photo by Marie Marcy.)

Pretty Woman

This collage was inspired by Picasso's *Seated Woman*. The piece contains visual imagery of an upper-class woman who has just come back from shopping with a name-brand handbag, shopping bags, orchid flowers, and a bowl full of cherries around her in the high-end foyer. The details come together to tell a story in time.

Tools: *Watercolor, knife, scissors, glue, tweezer*
Techniques: *Painting, cutting, gluing*

Interview with **Sarah Suplina**

When and how did you start your paper art journey?

I started working with paper as a result of being bored with regular watercolors as I had been a traditional watercolorist for many years. Eight years ago, in the spirit of experimentation, I cut up one of my landscape paintings. Then I placed and layered the cut paper to create a whole new piece of art. The layered and cut paper provided so much texture and depth—I have been in love with paper art ever since.

Could you briefly describe your process of creating a paper artwork?

I start each piece with an idea and a desire to create a certain subject matter. I then research and sketch that particular subject. Since I paint all my own paper, I will paint a certain color or pattern, if needed. Following the cutting, layering, and gluing process, the last step in my process is to paint the details. That is how a snippet is born.

When and how did you find your style of combining watercolor and collage in paper art? What kind of exploration have you experienced?

I have found my style through experimentation, and just trying different techniques. My style has evolved quite a bit over the years from traditional watercolors to where I am now. I find that my style now is the purest it has ever been.

You are an artist and a teacher at the same time. What is the biggest difference between these two roles? How do you keep a balance between creating art and teaching?

The biggest difference between my two professions is simple—teaching is a selfless profession, and being an artist is a selfish one. I share my knowledge, enthusiasm, and support with my students. My time with them is all about their needs. However, my role as an artist is all about myself, creating my interests, visions, and passions. The two professions, as they are so different, balance each other out beautifully.

Animals, especially birds, can be seen in your artwork frequently. Why are you keen on depicting them?

I love nature and everything about it: the beauty, the surprises, the colors, and textures... I respect nature and want to represent that through my artwork.

How do you maintain your passion for paper art? Has there ever been a time when you were ready to take a break?

I have never wanted to take a break. In fact, I find the opposite issue—I never have enough time to do all that I want to do. The more art I make, the more I desire to make! My passion for paper art is endless.

Is there anything new that you would like to try?

I am very happy with my work right now and how my art is being received. Someday, I would love to create a large installation of my snippets that would be exhibited for many to see and appreciate. I would want this installation piece to be a homage to nature and its beauty as my work usually does.

What is the biggest challenge you have experienced in your career as a paper artist so far?

Finding a price point for paper art continues to be my biggest challenge. People love the work of paper cutting, but do not realize the time and effort that an artist has put into creating paper art. Paper art is much more time-consuming and difficult than people might expect.

Do you have any suggestions for those who are searching for a breakthrough in their paper art?

My number one suggestion is to follow your vision and passion and to be original. Art is about individuality and is an inner voice that helps to express one's self. Be brave to take the time and take the risks to pursue your own artistic journey.

Birds of New York

These three birds, the ruffed grouse (on page 118), the woodpecker (on the top of page 119), and the American kestrel (on the bottom of page 119), are included in Sarah's latest series "Birds of New York." To the New Yorker Sarah, it was pure joy to depict the beautiful birds around her and complete the collage with local New York flowers and spring buds.

Tools: *Watercolor, knife, scissors, glue, tweezers*
Techniques: *Painting, cutting, gluing*

For the Love of Cats

Sarah's idea behind this piece was simply to show her love of cats. The cats chosen were broad in scope from the mighty lion to the clever fishing cat. Originally on her Instagram, Sarah shared only a snippet of "For the Love of Cats" at a time. Day by day, more snippets were shown to complete the final collage. The process was similar to a story with different images unfolding to a completion.

Tools: *Watercolor, knife, scissors, glue, tweezers*
Techniques: *Painting, cutting, gluing*

Beach Collection One

"Beach Collection One" is part of a series of three beach collages, each of which focuses on displaying different and beautiful shells from around the world. Through this piece and also the whole series, Sarah wanted to capture the essence and beauty of a beach day, sharing the feeling of going to the beach with the viewers.

Tools: *Watercolor, knife, scissors, glue, tweezers*
Techniques: *Painting, cutting, gluing*

Yulia Brodskaya

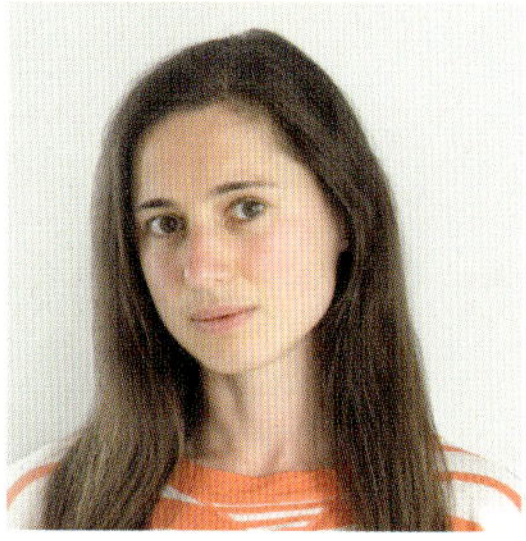

"The key is to enjoy the process; the rest will happen in its own time."

Yulia Brodskaya is a highly regarded paper artist known for her innovative approach to an ancient technique called "paper quilling." She uses two simple materials—paper and glue, and a technique involving the placement of carefully cut and bent strips of heavy paper. By making lush, vibrant, and three-dimensional paper artworks, she is pushing the boundaries of paper art.

Free Spirit

This is one of Yulia's self-initiated artworks featuring braids made of thin strips of soft card.

Tools: *Scissors, PVA glue*
Techniques: *Quilling, edge gluing, tearing paper to set the background*

Interview with **Yulia Brodskaya**

When and how did you start your journey of paper art?

About ten years ago, I was mainly interested in hand-drawn illustrations, especially letterforms. After working on them for a year or so, I decided to put together a promotional booklet that needed an eye-catching cover image. I tried to draw my name and put it on the cover, but none of the versions was good enough. Somehow, the idea of cutting a sheet of card into strips came to my mind. I began gluing these strips edges down, repeating the letter outlines. As the paper design of my name was ready, I realized that I was onto something very exciting. Immediately I dropped the illustrative booklet idea and immersed myself into this new world of paper instead.

Why is paper art special to you compared with other forms?

I love paper, and I believe that the possibilities of self-expression through paper and this particular technique are endless. I've just been scraping the surface and outlining the potential paths for other artists to follow and push this medium further.

Do you have any regular wells of inspiration?

I collect all sorts of beautiful photographs (mostly of nature and people) and browse through them from time to time. I look and observe with a clear mind and sometimes doodle. Quite often, ideas come in a form of hybrid visions when I draw elements from several different photo references all at once and combine them into a new unexpected artwork. I'm quite selective with my sketches or ideas—I will move to paper only when I feel eager to get started and strongly believe the sketch is worth the time.

The color of your artwork is very compelling. Do you have any tips for sorting out the palette?

The advice I often give is the same as what I taught my kids—think of a color scheme as a direction rather than an individual single color. For example, if you want to color something green, use as many tints and shades of green as possible. Richness and harmony of color palette come from there, not from using all colors from the rainbow. Restricting the number of hues and enriching the subtle color variations of each hue will help to achieve an attractive and harmonious color scheme.

What is the biggest difference between your recent works and those you created at the beginning of your experimentation with paper art?

My first projects were completely different from the large-scale portraits that I am working on. Mainly I focused on typography and decorative letters with paper strips. That was an essential period because my commercial work for editorial and advertising projects brought exposure and popularity to quilling and made it look modern and exciting. Therefore, there are more people practicing quilling these days than ten years ago.

My paper art is a reflection of my development as a person. Basically, it evolves naturally even though I have plans and clear ideas of where it's going. Following my heart and intuition, I allow these transformations to happen and come through.

How do you maintain your passion for paper art? Have you ever needed a break?

In the beginning, I thought that I would get bored after several years and switch to some other mediums. However, I only get more and more into it as 11 years have passed. It's an amazing feeling when you know that you are doing exactly what you are supposed to do. I get tired occasionally, but it's usually physical fatigue. After having a rest and spending time doing other things with my family, I'm eager to go back to paper artwork.

Any sage advice for those who are just starting to dive into the medium?

Just go for it without any worries. We become better at whatever we practice. Thus, every time a paper artwork is completed, you have learned something and will keep learning. The key is to enjoy the process; the rest will happen in its own time.

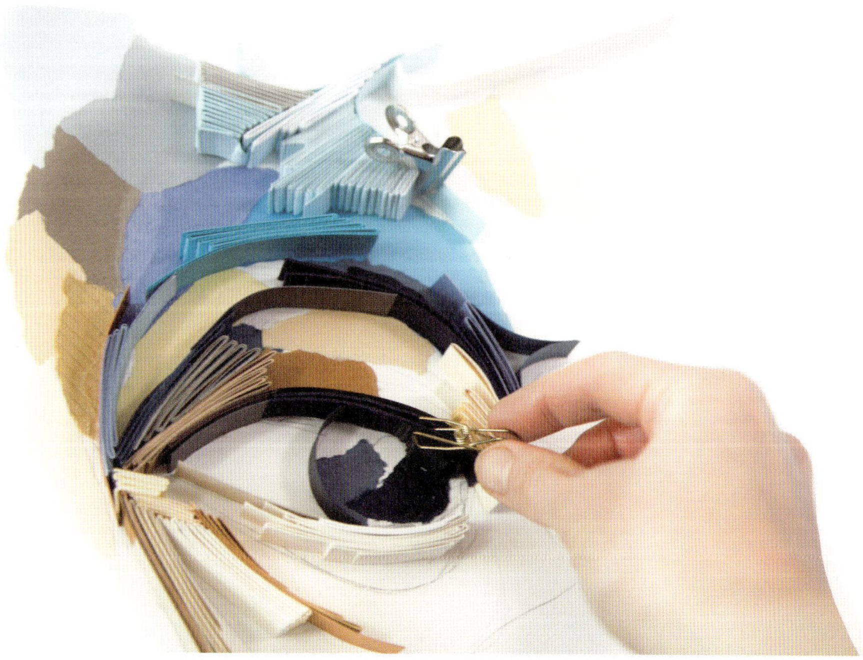

Pull to the Light

It is a large-scale portrait (1 m × 1.5 m) inspired by the invisible light and shine of positive energy.

Tools: *Scissors, PVA glue*
Techniques: *Quilling, edge gluing, tearing paper to set the background*

◂ Special Girl

This is an imaginary paper artwork superimposing a girl's face and hydrangea flowers.

Tools: *Scissors, PVA glue*
Techniques: *Quilling, edge gluing, tearing paper to set the background*

▴ Samurai Dreams

This is an imaginary portrait of an old *samurai*.

Tools: *Scissors, PVA glue*
Techniques: *Quilling, edge gluing, tearing paper to set the background*

◂ Van Gogh's Irises

This piece is the cover art for *The Artist's Magazine* with an assignment to re-create Van Gogh's famous painting *Irises* in paper.

Tools: *Scissors, PVA glue*
Techniques: *Quilling, edge gluing, tearing paper to set the background*

▴ Light Flower

It is a self-initiated piece sized 60 cm × 60 cm.

Tools: *Scissors, PVA glue*
Techniques: *Quilling, edge gluing*

Makerie Studio

"Paper always made sense to us—it is inexpensive and versatile, allowing you to shape it into almost anything with simple tools."

Makerie Studio is an award-winning creative workshop founded and run by Julie Wilkinson and Joyanne Horscroft. The studio designs and creates showpieces for window installations, advertising, editorials, and private collectors. Julie and Joy are inspired by forgotten worlds, rare prints, and the beauty of details, creating three-dimensional showpieces with uniquely developed techniques, precision, and passion.

International Women's Day Google Doodle

International Women's Day has significance for everyone regardless of gender. Believing that the freedoms they have enjoyed should be a right for all people, Makerie Studio represented this concept as a mandala, reminiscent of the planet we live on and of the life cycle we go through. At the center, they depicted some of the women who instigated the women's rights movement, which grew to include more women as this mandala does.

Tools: *Adobe Illustrator, Photoshop, scalpel, plotter, camera*
Techniques: *Cutting, scoring, layering, photographing*

When and how did you start your paper art journey?

We started around 2009 when we graduated from university and were still working on other jobs. We had always loved making and building things, but paper art was just a hobby. After a few long weekends spent making paper peacocks and cardboard buildings, we felt that it was time to try and do what we loved full-time.

Could you briefly describe your process of creating a paper artwork? Which part do you enjoy the most?

There are a few processes involved. The first step is to do research, collecting references, and understanding what exactly you want to make. Next, we draw up vectors of what we aim to build. When the vectors are ready, we cut all the pieces out and assemble them by hand, which is definitely the most fun part.

Why is paper art special to you compared with other forms of art?

Paper always made sense to us—it is inexpensive and versatile, allowing you to shape it into almost anything with simple tools. The process of seeing something flat turn into a three-dimensional sculpture is extremely satisfying, and being able to do that with just a scalpel and some glue is very inspiring.

Where do you usually get inspiration?

We get a lot of inspiration from architecture, antiques, and museum visits, as well as from other designers and artists. Sometimes we directly reference a part of something we've seen—a plaster church molding, or the shape of a staircase we like—but more often we use what we see to inspire new shapes and concepts for what we're building.

Have you ever experienced any creative block? How did you overcome it?

We've experienced plenty, particularly after long and intense projects which made us worn out. The best way to overcome it is often to allow yourself to switch off: close your laptop, take a deep breath, and stop trying to force your creativity. Go for a walk, visit a museum, allow your brain to completely relax, and focus on something else. Your creativity will always come back, it just needs some space.

Your artworks involve a fair amount of repeated patterns, very often circular, what is the fascination with these elements?

We love the predictability of circular patterns because they allow you to be as creative as you like while providing a fixed structure for the composition; we love the symmetry of them because they offer a beautiful visual pattern while still encouraging your eyes to move around them.

What is the most distinguishing feature of your work in your opinion?

Probably the intricacy of our artwork is the most distinct. We try and include decorative or patterned elements in most of our projects, and have become known for that aesthetic. We like people to look at our work and wonder how it's done. More is more and less is a bore!

Although the use of computer software continues to intrude into art and design, handcrafted work still excites people. What do you think are the qualities of paper art that makes it so timeless and powerful?

Craft and difficulty involved in handmade things probably will never be eclipsed by computer-generated work. Three-dimensional sculptures have a sensory quality that cannot be achieved by two-dimensional artworks, and this will continue to fascinate people regardless of (or perhaps in conjunction with) the advances in technology-based art. The sculpture also has a nostalgia about it that will forever be appealing, which is one of the reasons we love it.

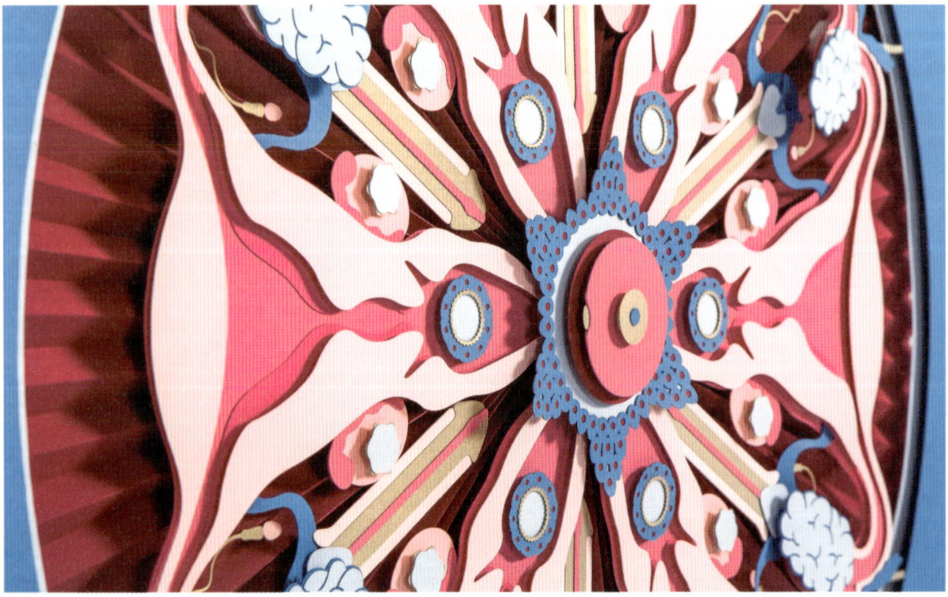

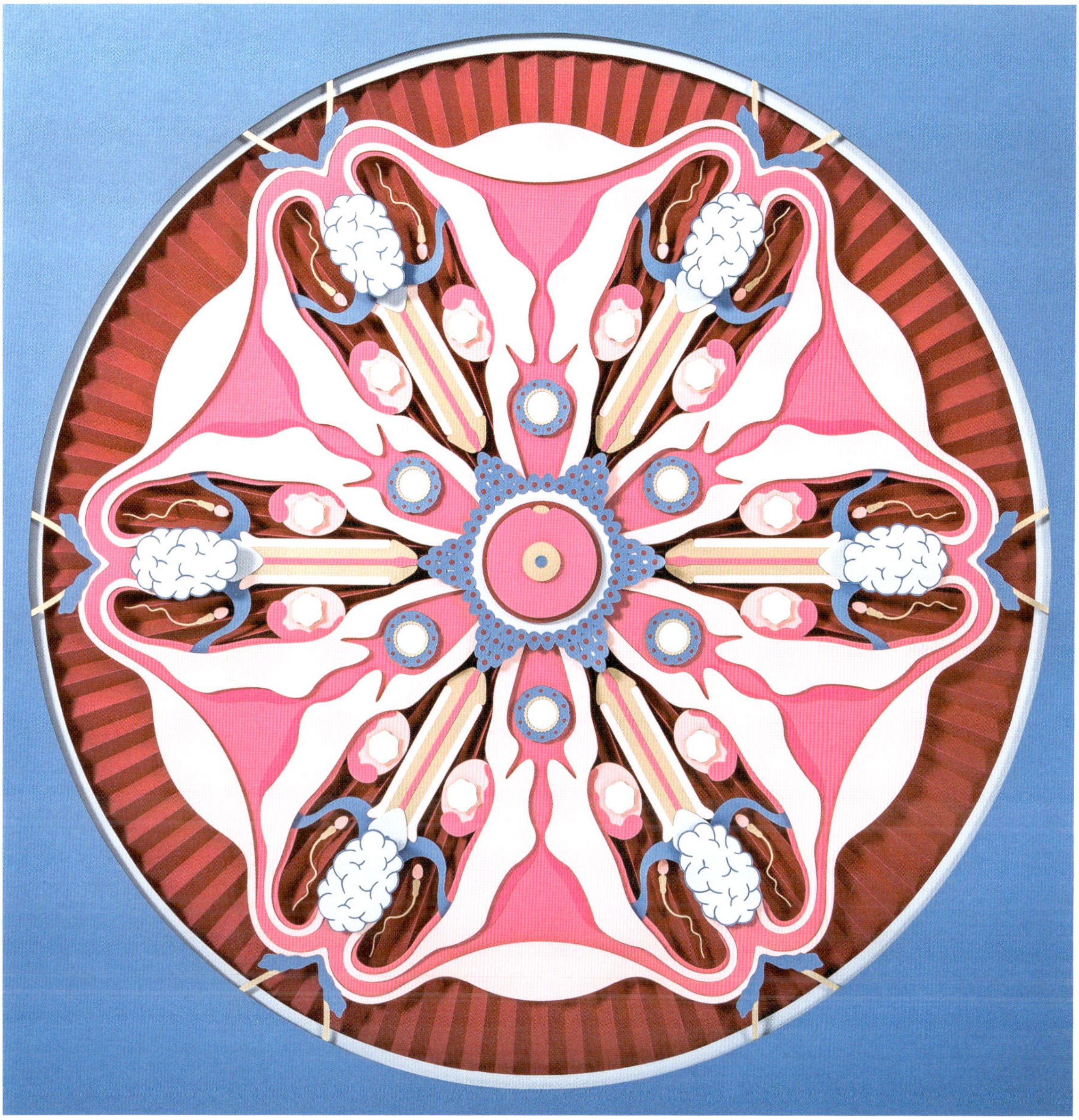

Manifestation

"Manifestation" is a personal project inspired by a long and intimate relationship with hypochondria. Started almost two years ago and informed by a lasting obsession with anatomy, this project was a way of providing a distraction from the various symptoms brought on by somatic symptom disorder. Performing practical tasks is an effective and productive way for Makerie Studio to avoid irrational health-related fears, particularly when focusing on the sources of the fears themselves.

Tools: *Adobe Illustrator, scalpel, plotter, camera*
Techniques: *Cutting, scoring, layering, photographing*

Circling

"Circling" is a personal project that comes from trying to deal with a period of fear and worry. Bright colors and happy thoughts are usually Makerie Studio's driving forces, but some days take their toll. Their way of dealing with anxiety and feeling less helpless is to make something constructive out of a stressful state of mind—turning darkness into beauty. Each piece is handmade using cut and layered iridescent gold and black paper.

Tools: *Adobe Illustrator, scalpel, plotter, camera*
Techniques: *Cutting, scoring, layering, photographing*

Entomologist

The detailed wings of the insects are delicate and intricate, multiplied to exaggerate the creature's original natural form. All pieces were cut from iridescent papers to create shimmering exoskeletons and faceted eyes, just like their living inspirations.

Tools: *Adobe Illustrator, scalpel, plotter, camera*
Techniques: *Drawing, cutting, photographing*

Photography: *Luke Kirwan*

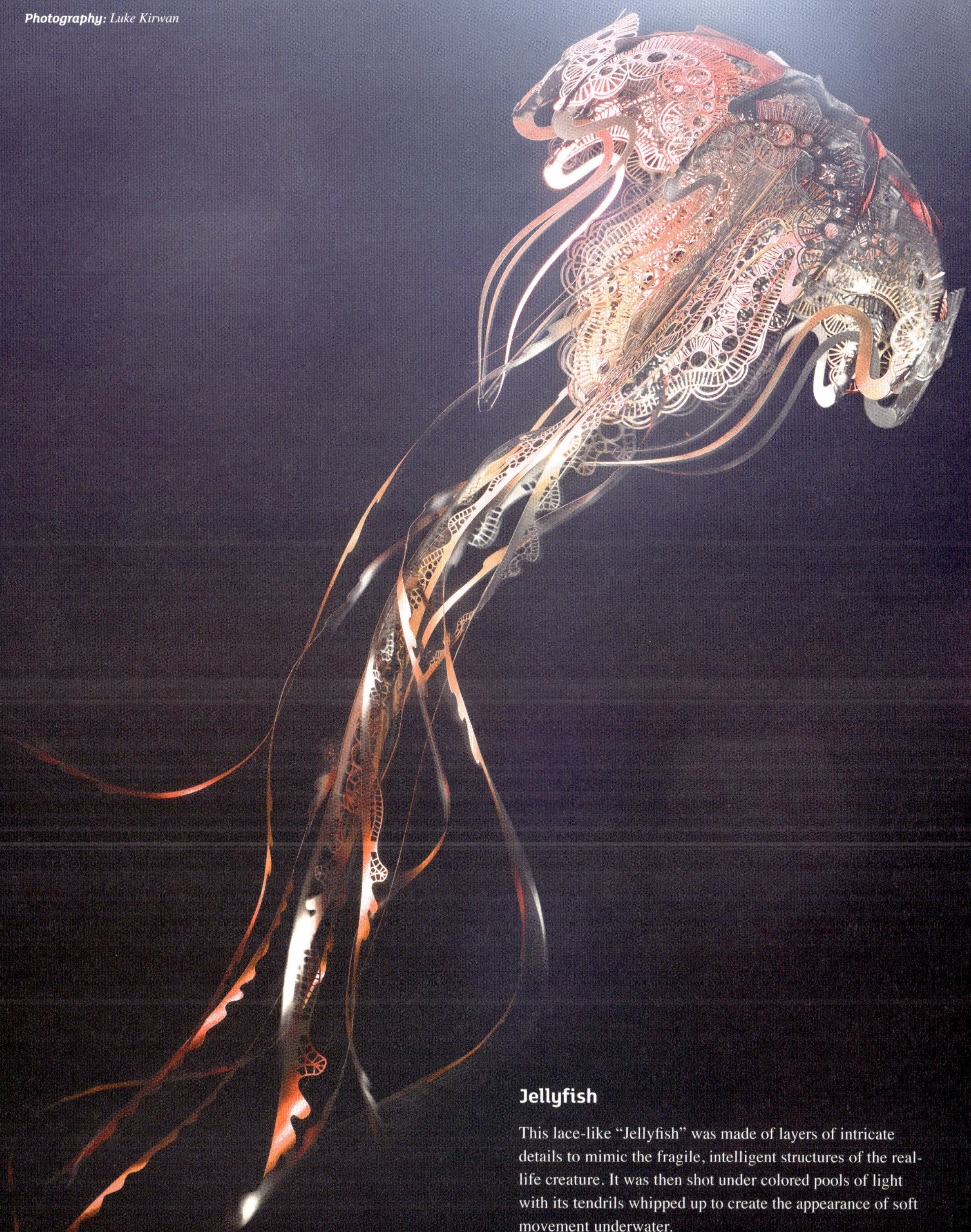

Jellyfish

This lace-like "Jellyfish" was made of layers of intricate details to mimic the fragile, intelligent structures of the real-life creature. It was then shot under colored pools of light with its tendrils whipped up to create the appearance of soft movement underwater.

Tools: *Adobe Illustrator, Photoshop, scalpel, plotter, camera*
Techniques: *Cutting, scoring, layering, photography*

Sena Runa

"Paper quilling is a relatively less known art, and I feel excited and happy to create something that has never been done before."

Having worked in human resources for seven years, **Sena Runa** became a full-time paper artist about five years ago due to her passion for art. With her unique, original, and colorful style, she enjoys spreading joy through her work around the world. Her tutorial book, *Quilling Art*, was translated into Dutch and Chinese, appealing to quilling lovers worldwide.

I am Turtley in Love with You

Turtles are one of the most vulnerable species because of global warming. This project depicts a sea turtle with the aim of attracting attention to environmental issues. In the shell of the turtle, the strips of paper were folded while strips in the other parts were quilled.

Tools: *Scissors, paper strips, glue, tweezers*
Techniques: *Cutting, folding, quilling, gluing*

Interview with **Sena Runa**

How did you decide to quit your job and become a full-time artist?

In 2012 when I was searching the Internet for inspiration to find the right hobby for me, I found a colorful picture that was made of paper using the quilling technique. Then I tried to make it myself with the color paper for *origami*. Although I was not so successful at the beginning, I found my own style after trying many times. Since then, my friends and family had asked me to make some pieces for them. It was at that moment that I started to consider working on quilling art as a career and decided to give it a try.

Could you briefly describe your process of creating a paper artwork?

Having settled on what I am going to visualize, I draw a template and choose the color scheme. After this, any further details are spontaneous, so the creative process of each item is slightly different. It takes approximately a day to complete one piece, and it might take longer to come up with something new.

Why is paper art special to you compared with other forms? And why do you prefer the technique of quilling?

I feel very comfortable while I am doing something with paper. One of the best parts is being able to create very colorful creations that make myself and other people feel good. It is a relatively little known art, and I feel excited and happy to create something that has never been done before. Also, I am trying new things such as combining drawing with paper quilling, which leads me to new paths.

Do you have any reliable sources of inspiration?

Although I work from home, I love nature and get inspiration from a blue sky, a tree, the ocean, and various things in the natural world. Besides, everyday things such as a magazine, a cup of coffee, and a song can inspire me. Sometimes people ask me to create something I have never thought of before, which helps me to find new inspirations as well.

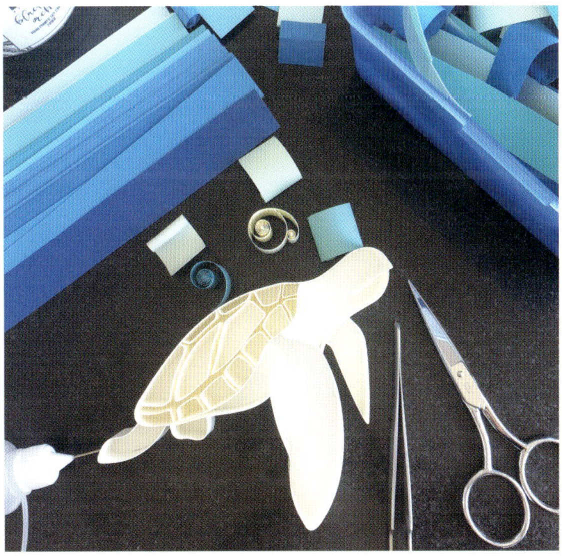

Have you ever experienced creative block? How do you overcome it?

I face this kind of problem in the creation process now and then. Usually, I take a break from an hour to several days. Having a break helps me to make decisions about whether to continue working on the artworks without any changes or make a change, if so, what kind of changes I should make.

Are there common themes of your artworks? What do you want to express through them?

I involve various subjects in my artworks without limits—heart-shape patterns, different animals and flowers, hot air balloons, world maps, and so on. Coloring everything and adding my point of view to my artworks make me feel good. I believe, in this way, I am spreading joy and cheerfulness to other people, which is my purpose while making art.

Is there anything new that you would like to try?

I want to concentrate on commercial projects which are becoming more and more important to me. New demands and collaboration offers that I didn't think about before sometimes broaden my horizon and drive me to think beyond the usual way. Besides, publishing my new tutorial book and creating bigger artworks are also in my plans.

Could you give some suggestions to those who just started to dive into paper art?

What I can suggest is to start any kind of art if you have a passion for it. You can find your own techniques and styles by trying again and again. Practicing will make the results much more satisfactory. Never try to copy other artists or creations because it would never give you joy as much as your own creations will do.

Poppy

Inspired by nature, this project is more than a quilling artwork because Sena used more folded paper strips than paper rolls to show the details of the flower. For the base of the flower, a large color range of markers were used.

Tools: *Copic markers, scissors, paper strips, glue, tweezers*
Techniques: *Painting, cutting, folding, quilling, gluing*

Day & Night

In this small-sized project, Sena wanted to reflect the contrast between the day and the night. Apart from the paper quilling technique, different colors were used for the base—blue for the night, white for the cloud, and yellow for the sun.

Tools: *Scissors, paper strips, glue, tweezers*
Techniques: *Cutting, folding, quilling, gluing*

Space Rocket

In this project, Sena applied two techniques—quilling for the details of the rocket and cutting for the smoke and details of the outer space in the background.

Tools: *Scissors, paper strips, glue, tweezers, foam boards*
Techniques: *Cutting, folding, quilling, gluing*

María Laura Benavente Sovieri

"The warmth of the material, the vibrant colors, the ability to be modeled—these qualities of paper fascinate me. With paper, you can create anything."

Also known as Mililitros, **María Laura Benavente Sovieri** has a creative mind concerned with generating visual solutions. She works as a photographer and paper craft illustrator, combining photography and paper art subtly.

PAPELERIA

Fruit Posters

This is a personal project depicting fresh fruits. Based on the color schemes and flavors, María Laura created these fruits, flat laid and shot them from above.

Tools: *Glue, cameo silhouette, scissors, art knife, box cutter, folding bone, airbrush*
Techniques: *Gluing, cutting, folding, painting, photographing*

Interview with **María Laura Benavente Sovieri**

When and how did you start your journey of paper art?

Once I finished my fine arts degree, I was looking for professional opportunities. In 2011, I made an illustrated collaboration about "calories" for a magazine and decided to create my own paper models instead of photographing the real objects. That was how my first paper illustrations emerged.

Why is paper art special to you compared with other mediums?

The warmth of the material, the vibrant colors, the ability to be modeled—these qualities of paper fascinate me. With paper, you can create anything.

Could you describe your process of creating a paper artwork? Which part do you enjoy the most?

Usually, when I create a paper artwork, I look for photographic references and start sketching by hand to find the correct composition and relation between the elements. Then, I create the models in a simple three-dimension program and use another program to display the model. Finally, I cut my model with the cameo silhouette, assemble, and glue it. The part I enjoy most is assembling the set, creating the composition, and adding little details that bring the composition to life.

As a photographer and paper artist at the same time, how do you combine the two disciplines?

Paper and photography are a perfect combination. Photography is a determining factor in my paper illustrations since I play with lights and shadows to highlight the shapes of each object. Normally, I use strong and clear lighting. There is always a dominant light in charge of highlighting the shadows and volumes that provide three-dimensionality to the photographed model.

What is the most distinguishing feature of your work?

I value the vibrant color range and the imperfection of the handmade objects. More importantly, I prefer rounded finishes and try not to incorporate geometry, which is a frequently used style in paper craft. Thus, I think the soft and organic forms are the most distinguishing part of my artwork.

You have completed a lot of successful commissioned projects. What is the key to impressing your clients and conveying the brands' value?

I think my strong point is designing eye-catching images that impress the viewers. Also, my visual language adapts to advertising well.

What kind of difficulties have you experienced in your career as a paper artist? How did you overcome them?

After working as a professional paper artist for a long time, I found the commissioned works for companies sometimes frustrating since there is less freedom and the result is not as agreeable as expected. In some cases, my clients wanted me to repeat a formula that I was tired of. My way of overcoming them is to consider them from a positive point of view. Having these sorts of restrictions occasionally can be beneficial because they push me to rethink the subjects and seek a new approach to the commissions. When you are stuck in some way, these experiences surely will advance your work if you take them as opportunities to grow.

Is there anything new that you would like to try, or is there anything that you are working on and hope to improve?

I'd like to have more time to carry out my personal projects, more free and creative illustrations. I have done some this year, and in this process, I have discovered new techniques that will be reflected in my subsequent works. Also, I have been thinking about carrying out a project in the field of children's book illustrations.

Corelle

This is a paper craft for Corelle Dining campaign at Forsman & Bodenfors.

Tools: *Glue, cameo silhouette, scissors, art knife, box cutter, folding bone*
Techniques: *Gluing, cutting, folding, photographing*

Street Food Festival

Based in Strasbourg, France, Street Food Festival is an event with food, music, and all kinds of activities. María Laura created these paper models for the cover of *Street Bouche Food Festival Magazine* and the banner of its Facebook page in 2018.

Tools: *Glue, cameo silhouette, scissors, art knife, box cutter, folding bone*
Techniques: *Gluing, cutting, folding, photographing*

STREET
BOUCHE

Zooo Hotel Pattern Series Spring/Summer 2018

Zooo Hotel is a brand for mothers and daughters. Inspired by prints, María Laura created these paper patterns for the 2018 campaign of the brand.

Tools: *Glue, cameo silhouette, scissors, art knife, box cutter, folding bone*
Techniques: *Gluing, cutting, folding, photographing*

Diana Beltran Herrera

"Artists feed their practices from everyday experiences."

Diana Beltran Herrera is a designer and artist who works with ordinary materials such as wire, cardboard, plastic, and paper—the primary medium of her work. For Diana, the divide between humans and nature is too wide. Through her work, she aims to improve the relationship by highlighting elements of the natural world that are threatened, overlooked or forgotten.

European Robin

"European Robin" was created specifically for the Leuchtendroter hotel in Frankfurt. By making several models, Diana wanted to capture the movements of the birds and show the changes in their chubby bodies.

Tools: *Scissors, watercolor, ink, glue, wire, tape, Adobe Illustrator, Photoshop*
Techniques: *Painting, cutting, gluing*

Interview with **Diana Beltran Herrera**

When and how did you start your journey of paper art?

I have been interested in paper since I was very little at kindergarten. Yet, paper art was not a career or profession for me until I graduated from design school. When I was searching for a job and wanting to be creative, I spent my days at home cutting and folding paper, exploring what could be done.

Have you ever experienced any creative block?

Actually, I find myself with lots of ideas and little time to visualize them all. I love to draw and write everything that goes on inside my head, thinking about my work or my ideas everyday. I also have different notebooks where I record my ideas and keep an archive of my work. Artists feed their practices from everyday experiences.

Many of your artworks revolve around animals, especially birds, why do you enjoy depicting them?

I like all kinds of things commonly seen in our daily life—animals are one of them. When I was in Finland, I noticed a magpie come to my studio every day, which caught my attention. It was my first time being outside of my country, so everything was new and exciting to me. I appreciated the close and harmonious relationship between nature and people in Finland, which allowed me to pay attention to things that I did not notice before. I became curious about how the birds inhabited the cities, such as how they found food and made houses. In order to know more about them without hurting or affecting them, I started making birds after learning about them. Making paper artworks is a way for me to learn and understand the things around me.

What is the relation between personal projects and commissioned projects for you?

Personal practice is important because it is an exploration where you learn what interests you as you improve yourself. For example, I collect various things, employ everyday materials, and replicate objects or shapes that I feel curious about. That's how I found some techniques and suitable materials. Then, in my commissions, I can apply all that I have learned during personal practice.

What is the biggest challenge you have experienced in your career as a paper artist?

Big projects and long-distance ones are definitely challenging. My biggest challenge so far was to design a shopping center installation in China. Since I was in England, the client and I communicated simply via email. I needed to design the models and provide instructions and visual images for a production company in China. Therefore, the material, measurements, and templates must be very clear visually so that what they came up with in the end would not look too different. It was very stressful but the production team offered a lot of help, which greatly reduced the pressure on me.

Is there anything new that you would like to try?

I am constantly trying different things on paper and love to research everyday materials, looking into my waste, and finding potential. Specifically, I hope to do more display windows and big installations that could integrate more elements. Also, I'd like to make more types of animals to develop new skills and techniques.

Could you give some suggestions to those who aspire for a breakthrough?

First, the desire to create something is important. Sometimes it takes a lot of effort to start because we want our ideas and results to be perfect. When the results ends up being different from our expectation, it can be de-motivating. So, my suggestion is to do some simple exercises regularly and have fun. I do take my work seriously but still enjoy the process, feeling excited to experiment and play with art. Besides, as I said before, record all the artworks you have done to see what you need to do to make them better. Finally, research as much as possible, look at what others are doing, fill yourself up with positivity and good energy so that inspiration will flow.

Singapore Children's Museum

In 2021, the former Singapore Philatelic Museum will reopen as the new Singapore Children's Museum. For this event, Diana was invited to exhibit her works and specially created new pieces of paper art depicting the local nature of Singapore. Additionally, stamps based on these pieces would be produced.

Tools: *Scissors, watercolor, ink, glue, wire, tape, Adobe Illustrator, Photoshop*
Techniques: *Painting, cutting, gluing*

Crimson
Sunbird
Aethopyga sipanaja
SINGAPORE
2007A
5
CENTS

Torch Ginger
Etlingera elatior
SINGAPORE
2007A
2ND
LOCAL

New Animals

In this project, Diana intended to create scenography and sets rather than simply the paper animals. With elements of their habitats around, the animals are placed in scenes instead of a blank background.

Tools: *Scissors, watercolor, ink, glue, wire, tape, Adobe Illustrator, Photoshop*
Techniques: *Painting, cutting, gluing*

Jackie Wen

"The only thing I believe would help to impress the audience is to create something impressive to myself first."

Born in Guangzhou, China, **Jackie Wen** is a paper artist specialized in installations. Apart from working with famous brands such as Nike, IKEA, and *National Geographic*, she has held three personal exhibitions and participated in a few group exhibitions in several different cities in China.

Blooming

In collaboration with the multi-media artist PD (Zhang Peiding), Jackie created this interactive paper installation. As the audience moves past the artwork, the paper flower blooms.

Tools: *Laser cutter, thread, glue*
Techniques: *Laser cutting, threading, gluing*

Interview with **Jackie Wen**

When and how did you start your paper art journey?

When I attended a course about book design at university, I became interested in paper and tried to create some projects with it for the course. After graduation, paper art was still one of my hobbies while I was working on other jobs. Four years later, I quit my job and decided to focus on creating paper art.

Why is paper art special to you as opposed to other mediums?

Paper is so ordinary that even small kids can create something with it by folding, cutting, and gluing. The most appealing thing about paper art is the uniqueness in this ordinariness—if you spend a lot of time working on it assiduously, you will accomplish a stunning artwork.

Where do you typically find inspiration? How do you transform the ideas into actual artworks?

Most of the inspirations are from my everyday life. Usually, I have a notebook with me and take notes of some ideas—could be a word, a sentence, or an image—that pop up anytime. When I am to start a new project, I will look back and pick some of the ideas to refine and visualize.

You have worked with many well-known brands. What's the key to impressing your clients and adding value to the brand?

I engaged in various design jobs after studying visual communication in college, and these working experiences enable me to balance the artistic and commercial part of my creation. Personal projects are mainly about expressing myself, and I don't have to consider much. For commercial collaboration, I usually conduct a lot of research on the background of the brand and the clients' demands, clarifying our mutual aim. Luckily, most clients gave adequate space for me to maintain my personality and style. Thus, I believe the key to an agreeable result is the trust between the artists and clients.

Many of your artworks are interactive. What does a successful interaction between the audience and the work look like?

Actually, I don't know how to define "success." The only thing I believe would help to impress the audience is to create something impressive to myself first. I enjoy seeing how the audience interacts with my artwork because they have different experiences and may resonate with it in different ways, which makes the artwork more "complete."

How did you find your stylistic voice with paper art? Is there a defining characteristic to your work?

The style of my artwork changes as my experience grows because each artwork has its life too. For instance, I mainly made small pieces at the beginning, but recently I am working on more large-scale installations. I think the audience is the one to define and categorize my style, and the only thing I need to do is to focus on creation without drawing lines to limit the possibilities.

Could you share one of your favorite paper artists?

I always appreciate Zim&Zou very much because they are good at blending various colors into one project harmoniously. They can handle a lot of fluorescent colors that I don't even dare to try. When viewing their works, I can't help being amazed at the gorgeousness of color.

Is there anything new that you would like to try?

I have tried to bring paper art into the water and suppose burning it would be a possible direction. I'd like to explore more interesting possibilities while creating interactive paper art as well.

Photography: *Frankie Yeung*

By Flow

In this project, Jackie brought paper art into the water, subverting the idea that paper and water cannot work well together. The relationship between the jellyfish and flow is a metaphor of the relationship between individuals and society—we seem to follow the trends unconsciously.

Tools: *Laser cutter, glue*
Techniques: *Laser cutting, jointing, gluing*

Midnight of the Quiet Sea

This project is an exploration of the mysterious creatures shining under the dark and quiet sea at night.

Tools: *Scalpel, LED lights*
Techniques: *Cutting, gluing*

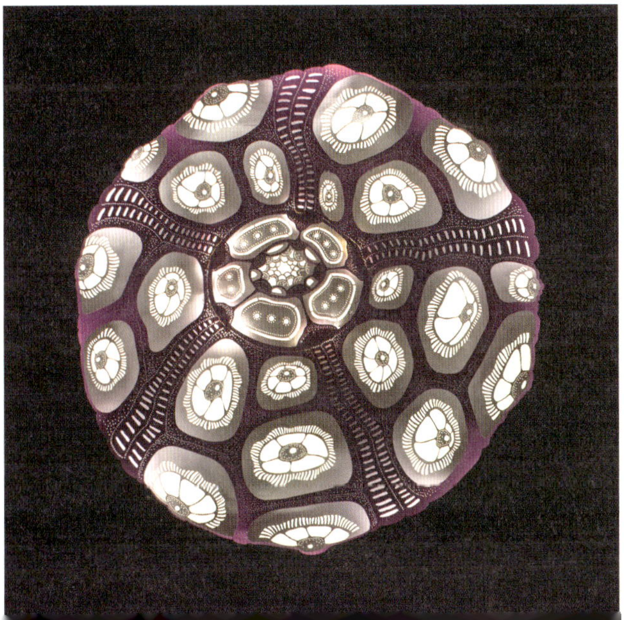

Zim&Zou

"It is the fragility of paper that gives a lot of poetry to an artwork, allowing it transcend the subject."

Zim&Zou is composed of two French artists, Lucie Thomas and Thibault Zimmermann. After studying graphic design for three years, they decided to focus on installations using handcrafted objects. Their favorite material is paper that they manipulate to give rise to intricate and colorful sculptures. Paper inspires them with its versatility, infinite range of colors, and unique textures.

Forest Folks

It is an artistic window display project for the opening of a new Hermès store in Dubai. In this project, "life" is everywhere—flowers are growing and carrying away the inhabitants in their impetus. These mysterious people are evolving, building, and living right in the heart of nature, revealing a fragment of their daily life.

Tools: *Cutter, ruler, compass, glue*
Techniques: *Cutting, folding, gluing*

Interview with **Zim&Zou**

When and how did you start your journey with paper art?

More than ten years ago, we worked separately for a few local clients, doing logotypes, branding, and other corporate designs using computers. Quickly, we felt something was missing. We desired to explore another field and have fun. As Zou's grandparents were working in a paper factory, we had access to a lot of unsold paper sheets, which we decided to use differently and sculpt a game boy out of. It was a total freestyle but we were happy with the result. That was the beginning of our trip!

Describe your process for creating paper art?

Firstly, based on the brief, we talk, read, and brainstorm, feeding our imagination with everything we can. Then we select the best three ideas to sketch and develop the one chosen by the client with more sketches, documentation, colorization, and so on. As paper art is time-consuming, any mistake or change of mind is hard to handle. Thus, we need things to be as clear as possible before production. Once everything is precise, we draw the pieces on the computer, then print, cut, and glue pieces by hand.

Why do you prefer paper as a medium?

We like paper because it is common and affordable. This material has a countless number of colors, textures, weights, opacities, patterns, and so on. Meanwhile, its fragility pushes the artist to concentrate and to be respectful of the material. It is the fragility of paper that gives a lot of poetry to an artwork and transcends the subject.

You have completed some very successful commissioned projects. Is there a key to satisfying your clients and conveying the brands' value?

We think that the secret of satisfying a client relies on the following two points. Firstly, you should listen to the client's brief as it is the base of the artwork, then you need to devote yourself to the project. We are lucky because now our clients come to us for the "Zim&Zou" style, giving us enough space to express ourselves.

What is the best thing about working as a duo?

Being a creative duo and also a couple, we know each other well. We're similar but different. Even if we have the same way to approach a subject, we have to convince each other that an idea works. Sometimes you have to admit that your partner is right, which reminds you to stay humble and serve the project only. Therefore, the best thing is to confront your ideas and justify everything to help the project go further. It is this unique alchemy that makes each of our projects special.

What was the biggest challenge you have experienced in your career as paper artists?

We had experienced a lot of challenges. For example, the most important challenge we were confronted with recently was a huge window display for the opening of a new Hermès boutique. The main window ran on two stairs (at an angle), so we had to make a paper building as high as five meters! Thanks to the local team, the result was really impressive.

Art and design are increasingly done using computer software, but handcraft still fascinates many people. What are the qualities of paper art that make it so timeless?

We love digital designs, but we feel that creating artworks using real materials is more tactile, or even more "sensual." That's personal, but the happiness and satisfaction we have after a big project are so much stronger. Watching the installation from different angles is also very pleasant—it reacts to different lightings, reminding us of all the small stories we have with each element when composing the artwork. Although paper sculpture is best seen in person, viewers can still feel the texture, even in a picture.

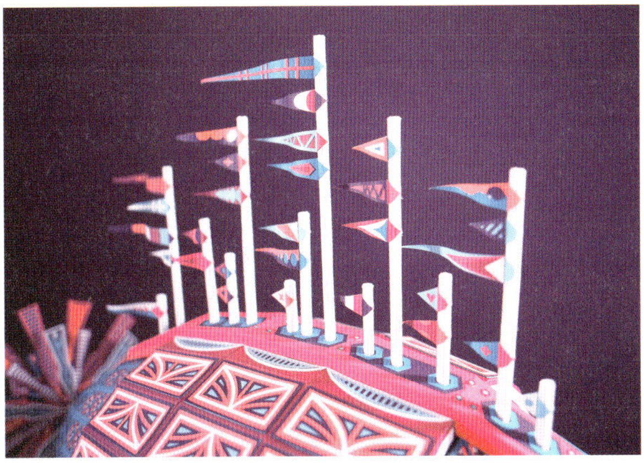

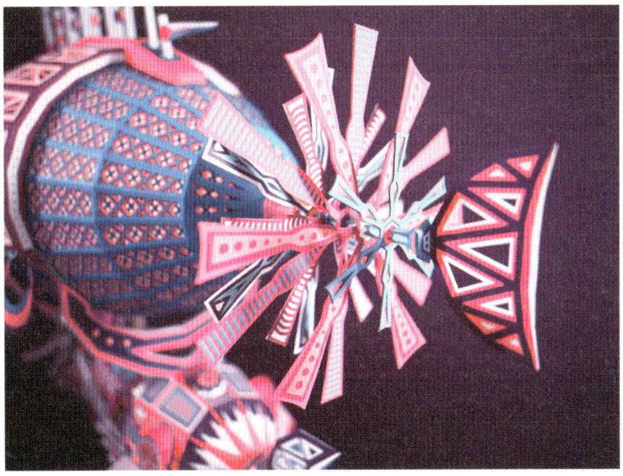

EXODUS

"EXODUS" is an ode to travel. Thrown in an endless movement, the aircraft colony crosses time and space toward an unknown outcome. Like birds stuck in an eternal migration, they are pursuing their dream of somewhere else.

Tools: *Cutter, ruler, compass, glue*
Techniques: *Cutting, folding, gluing*

Sharing Worlds: *One Hundred Years of Solitude*

"Sharing Worlds" are two pieces of paper art created for an exhibition of the Nobel Prize Museum in Dubai, based on two books that won the Nobel Prize for Literature. One of them, for *One Hundred Years of Solitude* written by Gabriel Garcia Marquez, published in 1967, focuses on the house where the whole story takes place. The house, isolated from the crowd and surrounded by vegetation, is almost hidden from the world. Small key recurring elements of the story are also hidden in the dense vegetation around the house.

Tools: *Cutter, ruler, compass, glue*
Techniques: *Cutting, folding, gluing*

Sharing Worlds: *Kristin Lavransdatter*

The other, treated as a landscape, is for *Kristin Lavransdatter* written by Sigrid Undset, published in 1920. It is a tribute to the Norway of the 14th century. The scene is taking place around Trondheim Cathedral which is a key location in the story.

Tools: *Cutter, ruler, compass, glue*
Techniques: *Cutting, folding, gluing*

Paper Barcelona

This artwork is a creation of a paper city, inspired by Barcelona. The most iconic buildings characterizing Barcelona's landscape are regrouped in a single installation. The architectural details are interpreted into "flat" sculptures.

Tools: *Cutter, ruler, compass, glue*
Techniques: *Cutting, folding, gluing*

Photography: *Philippe Moraiz*

Estudio Guardabosques

"It is great that we, as artists, can use our tools to introduce all these species in nature to people."

Based in Buenos Aires, **Estudio Guardabosques** is a studio formed by graphic designer Carolina Silvero and audiovisual designer Juan Elizalde, who work in design, illustration, and art direction mainly with paper craft. (Portrait photo by Guille Vizzari.)

Type Design: *Yani&Guille*

Home Hotel exhibition

Invited to exhibit in the amazing Home Hotel in Buenos Aires by Fabian Trigo, Estudio Guardabosques took the opportunity to try new things. They designed a series of dioramas based on their beloved naturalists and astronomers—David Attenborough, Carl Sagan, John James Audubon, and Grizzly Man's Timothy Treadwell.

Tools: *Paper, plotter cutter, glue*
Technique: *Paper crafting*

Interview with **Juan Elizalde** at **Estudio Guardabosques**

When and how did you start your journey with paper art?

We met in 2011 and started collaborating on some experiments. In 2012, some friends offered to make an exhibition of our work. That exhibition, with the theme of nature, was named "Guardabosques" (forest rangers) and mainly featured paintings, paper sculptures and cuttings. After that, we kept experimenting with paper, finding new challenges and showing our art on the Internet, which led to further commercial and personal projects. We kept "Guardabosques" as our nickname for a few projects, and then it became the name of our studio.

What is the best thing about working as a duo? How do you cooperate and divide the work?

Although we don't think in exactly the opposite way, we have different points of view. During every project, we have a lot of discussions, that greatly optimize the final product. Our favorite projects are those in which we can identify different elements contributed by each of us. Regarding the division of work, both of us do everything all the time, from producing to designing to cutting the material. Yet, I often work more on the three-dimensional designs and templates while Carolina focusses more on the final assembly and aesthetic fine-tuning.

Why is paper art special to you?

We don't know exactly, but one thing is for sure—paper has become part of our life, and we love to experiment with it to see how far we can go. Even after working with paper for around ten years now, we still feel excited to make paper sculptures with our own hands and to see the finished projects.

You have delivered a lot of successful commissioned projects. Could you share the key to bringing value to a brand and impressing your clients?

We are not sure about that but something very important in our works is to build trust and respect with our clients. Our favorite and best-looking projects were created when the clients trusted us to propose our own vision of the work, in which we mostly tried to include nature as the subject. Thus the key may be to trust your vision and push it when possible. As you keep working on different projects, most of them will have some personal touches and become your style. That's what clients are looking for, at least in our case.

How did you arrive at your style of paper art? What is the most distinguishing feature of your work?

We work mainly in a low-poly style, making paper faceted sculptures with the least facets possible. Following this style, we started to experiment on two different paths: One was to reduce the facets at a minimum, and the other to add more facets and details to push the boundary. Both paths contributed to expanding our style. We reckon that our most distinguishing feature could be the attention to details in the animals that we represent. We draw inspiration from nature, obsessed with representing its subjects as faithfully as possible, not just with a superficial or thematic approach.

Many of your artworks involve nature, would you mind expounding on this fascination?

When Guardabosques just started, I was studying natural sciences which influenced the subjects we chose to portray. Nature is infinite, so we can keep learning, discovering, and getting fascinated by new animals, plants, insects, fungi, and so on. There is something aesthetic in nature which we enjoy rendering as we love seeing the representations of other artists such as Ernst Haeckel, Charley Harper, and Karl Blossfeldt. It is great that we, as artists, can use our tools to introduce all these species in nature to people.

Computer software is increasingly prevalent in developing contemporary art and design, but many people are still attracted to handcraft. What do you think are the qualities of paper art that makes it powerful and timeless?

Paper being such an everyday material, it's always surprising and exciting to see unexpected art coming from it. Of course, you can appreciate it in photos, but seeing a paper sculpture or paper cutting in real life always adds an extra layer of goodness. Also, working in crafts is a different mental process, not only because of having less screen time but because of the intimate connection between yourself and what you're doing by hand. That's one of the reasons we started designing our collections of paper kit products.

Museo del Humor Exhibition: Urban Mutations

Estudio Guardabosques was invited to participate in the "Mutaciones Urbanas" (Urban Mutations) exhibition at the Museo del Humor in Buenos Aires with an assignment to interpret the Natural Museum of La Plata under a futurist context. Mixing a Japanese element of *kaiju* (monster) and the idea of natural science of researching unknown species, the two artists gave rise to this friendly mutant monster named Musgor and the bugs that inhabit his body.

Tools: *Paper, plotter cutter, glue*
Technique: *Paper crafting*

Oni

After traveling to Japan, the two artists wanted to design something related to the amazing Japanese culture. As Juan has been fascinated with *yokai* (monster, specter) for a while, he started with an *oni* (devil).

Tools: *Paper, plotter cutter, glue*
Technique: *Paper crafting*

Photography: *Andrés Aguiló*

Rosa Yoo

"Paper is indeed a common material, but its creative potentials are endless in the hands of artists."

Rosa Yoo has been working as a paper artist since winning the prize in a paper art contest in 2009. She is interested in three-dimensional paper illustration and has held several exhibitions and taught a few workshops.

Autumn Mood Pumpkins!

Autumn, the season of fruiting, is usually connected with harvested pumpkins. Along with the paper pumpkins, the mini houses and the background are also painted in pumpkin color to create an autumn mood.

Tools: *Knife, glue, tweezers, bone folder*
Techniques: *Cutting, folding, gluing*

Interview with **Rosa Yoo**

When and how did you start your relationship with paper art?

Years ago, I saw dinosaur models made of paper on display at a large bookstore. Next to it was a DIY paper craft book issued by a Japanese publisher, which contained three-dimensional templates for a number of dinosaur models. That day, I bought the book and came home and made all the dinosaurs included, staying up all night for several days. Perhaps it was the dinosaurs that led me to the journey of paper art.

Could you briefly describe your process of creating an artwork?

When a good idea comes to me, I first make a sketch and take note of the things I need to keep in mind. Next, I make a template based on the sketch. Since I can hardly preview the three-dimensional result in my head, making a sample to test the template is necessary. In this way, the template can be adjusted immediately if there are any problems. Once the template is modified, I cut the parts one by one and assemble them with glue.

Why is paper art special to you?

It is really interesting to me that paper is indeed a common material, familiar to both children and adults, but its creative potentials are endless in the hands of artists. Paper is so strong and versatile and the diversity of its texture and color is beyond our imagination.

Have you ever experienced any creative block? How did you overcome it?

I think most artists would experience a creative block at least once, and I am no exception. I have several ways to overcome it, one of which is visiting a paper shop. While I am looking at and touching different types of paper, ideas of new pieces of paper art emerge. The other way is to take a break from paper. Contradictorily, when I am not so eager for ideas or inspiration, creative sparks come back to me.

Many of your artworks involve mini houses and furniture, why are they attractive to you?

I do enjoy creating mini-size works. These artworks are inspired by what we can see in our everyday life. By adding various details referencing the real world, I try to give them liveliness. The objects are made so small that they can be placed in a box, a glass dome, or a frame with depth, showing a scene of people's daily life. Making these mini artworks allows me to view everything around me from a different perspective with warm eyes.

Your artwork is colorful. Do you have any techniques or tips for choosing the palette?

I love colorful artworks. At the stage of sketching for a work, I make a color palette to determine the tone of the work. Overall, the color combination is one of the important elements that reveal the meaning of the work. Choosing the right colors is tricky and time-consuming but fun. To find out more beautiful and unique color combinations, I try to memorize various colors in my daily life. For example, I am impressed and inspired by the colors of some visually stimulating magazines and books, works from other artists on the Internet, and outfits of my friend who is a fashionista. The more attention that I pay to the colors around, the more I'll be able to develop a sense of choosing the perfect combination.

How did you find your style of paper art? Is there a single most distinguishing feature of your work?

In my opinion, the keywords of my work are three-dimensional, detailed, and real. Strangely, I do not have much interest in making two-dimensional works with paper. Instead, I am fond of turning the two-dimensional paper into wonderful three-dimensional works through the process of cutting, folding, and assembling, which is kind of magic to me. I tried to learn different types of techniques and applied them to many of my artworks. It took a long time and a lot of practice, but now I am satisfied with my own way of making the paper objects real through three-dimensional techniques and details.

Hello Spring!

The gardening items are placed side by side to celebrate the coming of spring. And mainly pink and green tones are used to create the warmth and freshness of spring.

Tools: *Knife, glue, tweezers, bone folder*
Techniques: *Cutting, folding, gluing*

▲ **Blue Christmas**

The common colors seen on Christmas are red and green, but Rosa created an unusual mini living room in a blue tone for Christmas.

Tools: *Knife, glue, tweezers, bone folder*
Techniques: *Cutting, folding, gluing*

▸ **Winter Night**

With these empty chairs, Rosa aimed to depict two persons sitting face to face and talking to each other by the fireplace at winter night. This paper miniature is so tiny that it fits inside the eyeglasses frame.

Tools: *Knife, glue, tweezers, bone folder*
Techniques: *Cutting, folding, gluing*

Christmas Tree

Knolling is one of Rosa's favorite ways of photographing. Rather than hanging on a tree, these tiny paper items are flat-laid to form the shape of a Christmas tree.

Tools: *Knife, glue, tweezers, bone folder*
Techniques: *Cutting, folding, gluing*

Cotton Candy Shop

Hanji is a type of traditional Korean paper made from mulberry wood. By scratching the surface of it, Rosa used *hanji* to present the soft texture of cotton candy.

Tools: *Knife, glue, tweezers, bone folder, hanji*
Techniques: *Cutting, folding, gluing*

If You Stay with Me Just Once in a While, I Won't Be Afraid of My Everyday Voyage

Through the long title and the three-dimensional paper illustration, Rosa wanted to deliver the message that life is an everyday voyage.

***Tools:** Knife, glue, tweezers, bone folder*
***Techniques:** Cutting, folding, gluing*

Sam Pierpoint

"I love creating little worlds where viewers can actually look around the elements and look inside of the windows."

Sam Pierpoint is a Bristol-based image-maker and art director specializing in creating handcrafted paper sets and sculptures. She designs, cuts, and handcrafts her creations from a range of sustainable materials. Her paper sculptures are used both commercially and artistically for a variety of applications such as advertising and packaging.

Photography: *Mike Foyle*

Soho House

House Notes is published each month by Soho House, a worldwide chain of boutique hotels and members' clubs. Sam was asked to create a sculpture for the cover of its Christmas edition as well as on a three-page spread within the magazine. With locations spanning everywhere from the British countryside to the West Coast of America, the idea behind this cover is to depict the variations of the members' clubs around the world.

Tools: *Silhouette Studio software, Silhouette Cameo, G. F Smith paper, craft knife, UHU glue*
Techniques: *Drawing, cutting, gluing*

Could you briefly describe your process of creating a paper artwork?

Most of the time, my process starts with a small thumbnail sketch which, following client's feedback, develops into a more detailed sketch and color palette. After that, I scale things up and plan on building the sculpture. Once I've got my scaled-up measurements, I build the base of the structure with the necessary platforms for the buildings to sit on and adjust their positioning to have the composition look close to the final sketch. Then I build the landscape and begin making templates on the Silhouette Studio software. These details are then cut out on a cutting machine and assembled carefully by hand. The next stage is the project photography which we often do in-house. I'm very lucky to work at a home studio with my partner who is a photographer and videographer. Over the years we've developed a style of post-processing that really brings the work to life.

What do you love about paper?

It's a material that I'm naturally drawn towards because I wanted my drawings to come to life off the page. I love creating little worlds where viewers can actually look around the elements and look inside of the windows. A big part of my work is focused on the environment so I use G. F Smith's recycled paper which offers an organic handmade aesthetic to my artworks of campaigns and set design.

You have delivered some successful commissioned projects. How does that differ from your process for personal projects?

Since I love following a brief, I think clear communication is the key to creating a successful image that works for the client and the artist as well. In my spare time, I usually work on personal projects. It's such an important thing to do as the personal projects help shape the direction I want to push my work in.

What are some of the challenges of trying to make a career out of paper art?

The biggest challenge has been finding ways to keep high-quality-looking work but, at the same time, cut the making time to fit into tight deadlines. I still haven't worked it out completely, and there have been many times when I stayed up so late to complete the work on time. I have made it easier for myself by finding great assistants who can help out when I have a big project. Also, I'm currently learning about different three-dimension software that might help with building geometric shapes more efficiently.

Do you have any suggestions for those looking to breakthrough in paper art?

It is necessary to keep experimenting and playing with paper until you find a unique style. Besides, knowing a good photographer is helpful. Without having quality photos, it's difficult to show your amazing work to attract more viewers. Even if hiring a professional photographer is too expensive, finding a student who is on a photography course would also work well, which provides an opportunity for you two to help each other out and make progress together.

Is there anything new that you are trying?

Yes, I'm currently working with my partner on an animated paper sculpture for an environmental campaign. Animation is something we'd like to do much more of. Also, I am working on three-dimension software like Blender to come up with complicated templates which will help to save a lot of time.

Our Responsibility

This artwork (on the left of page 214) was created for an art auction held by the design agency Accept and Proceed. It was the first time when some of the most influential and game-changing graphic designers, artists, and innovators got together to represent the truth around climate change. The proceeds were donated to Extinction Rebellion.

Tools: *Silhouette Studio software, Silhouette Cameo, G. F Smith paper, craft knife, UHU glue, Dispa board, netting*
Techniques: *Drawing, cutting, gluing*

Penguin, Sloth

"Penguin" and "Sloth" (on the right of page 214) are taken from two bigger projects respectively.

Tools: *Silhouette Studio software, Silhouette Cameo, G. F Smith paper, craft knife, UHU glue, paper strips for the interior*
Techniques: *Drawing, cutting, gluing*

Earth Hour

Earth Hour is the first step towards making nature matter. Millions of us around the world turn our lights off as a symbol of our commitment to the planet. This piece of paper artwork, with a TV screen shining behind, is the main part of an experimental animation to celebrate and hopefully help increase the awareness of Earth Hour.

Tools: *Silhouette Studio software, Silhouette Cameo, G. F Smith paper, craft knife, UHU glue*
Techniques: *Drawing, cutting, gluing*

Floral Head

This piece is one of the three editorial illustrations for the Alumni Publication of St. Edwards University in Austin, Texas.

Tools: *Silhouette Studio software, Silhouette Cameo, G. F Smith paper, craft knife, UHU glue*
Techniques: *Drawing, cutting, gluing*

Sara Rayo

"With the theme of geometry and natural forms, I want to express how nature is inherent in everything and how everything is perfect and not random on a microscopic level."

By investigating the microscopic forms of diatoms and other imperceptible creatures of the ocean, **Sara Rayo** has discovered an entirely different realm of geometry that spans the smallest atom to the most remote galaxies in our universe. Through paper sculptures, she tries to extrude and dimensionalize the flat surface of geometry that she has found in nature.

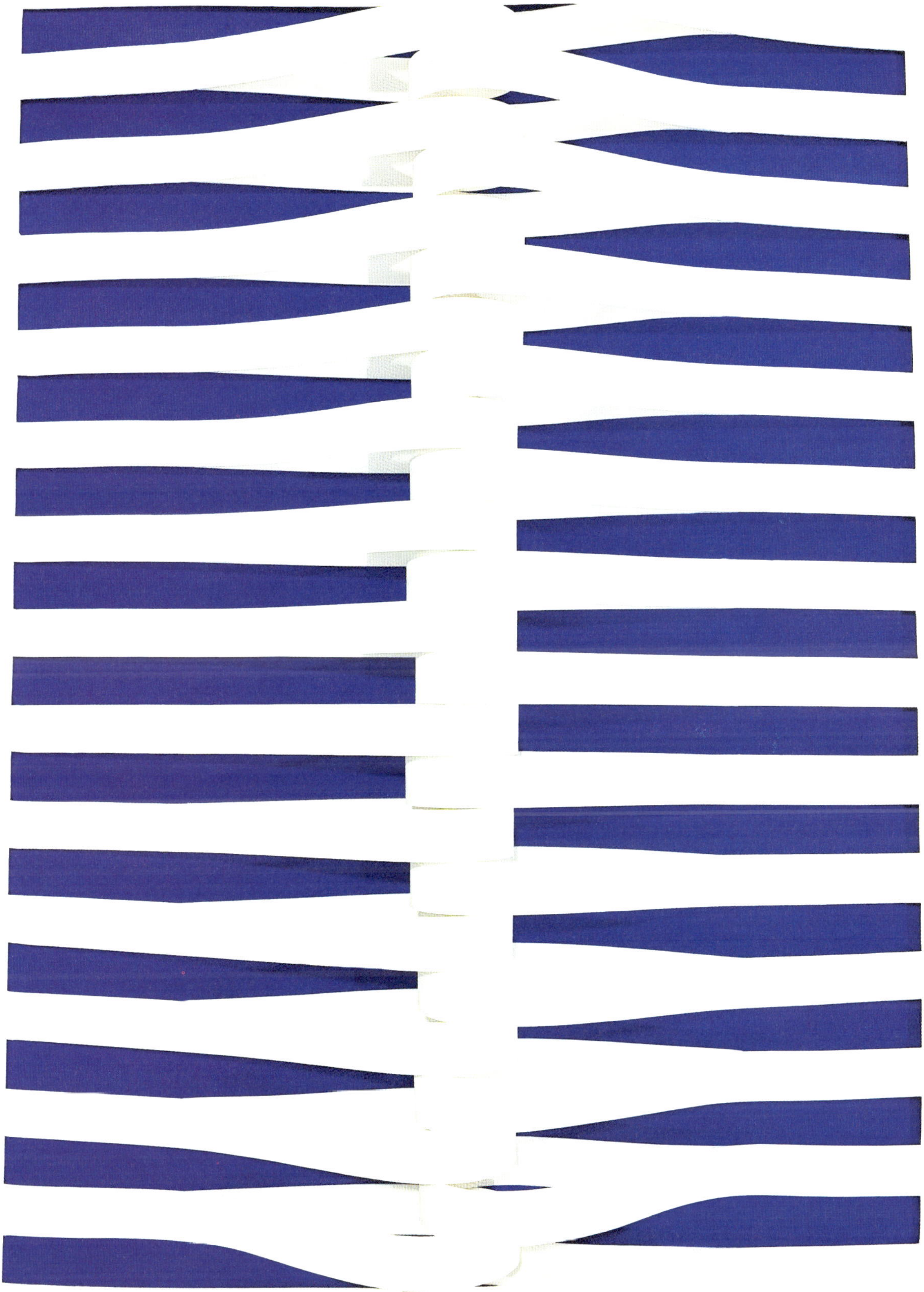

Androgynous Flower

This piece was inspired by the different carnivorous flowers in the tropics. How delicate yet strong they are while simultaneously manifesting aggression and submission! The strong colors in the interior convey a tropical thorn vibe while the purity of the white surface expresses calmness.

Tools: *300 lb paper, knife, PVC glue*
Techniques: *Cutting, bending, gluing*

When and how did you start your journey with paper art?

My father who was also an artist used to work with paper printing and intaglio, so I have handled and worked with paper since I was a child. That's why I understand the feeling and structure of paper—in other words, its soul. I have always been drawn to paper and enjoy staying long hours looking at paper in the paper store and feeling the different textures under my fingertips.

Would you mind sharing your process of creating a paper artwork?

My process begins with an investigation into color patterns and microscopic forms in nature as well as reviews of my finished work. The selection of the paper and the size is the specific part that I enjoy since I can look at the blank pieces of paper before they become three-dimensional. Then in the cutting part, I feel my essence is engrained into the paper. To cut such thick paper, I need bright light, a sharp knife, a steady hand and, most importantly, total concentration. After the folding, pulling, and opening of the cut pieces, my artwork starts to take form and become real. Later, I glue and polish the pieces to finish it off. Sometimes I unglue, re-glue, move, and change the pieces depending on how I feel. In the end, I set it into a frame to display it.

Many of your artworks involve patterns, is there a reason for this preference?

I feel there is a calming effect from looking at patterns. Repetition, similar to rhythm, creates movement and unity. Pattern and repetition are found in nature in many forms, telling a visually intriguing story that draws the audience into the work. For example, the golden ratio is found in nature and then used in art. All of the alike things that can be referenced as patterns in one way or another are an important part of my work.

How did you come up with the idea of combining light and paper art?

Since my creations are three-dimensional with many layers, each layer of my artworks needs light in order to be seen. By adding light, I am able to illuminate the interior, showing the depths of the work.

Is there anything new that you would like to try?

My work is getting more and more geometric. I can't tell exactly where it will end up but I see more precision and calculations happening as I work, feeling the gravitational pull towards more rigor and meticulousness. Although my work ranges within many sizes and dimensions, I'd like to try even larger-scale work, exceeding ten feet or more, which may have to become modular due to the limit of the size of a paper sheet.

Is there a singularly stunning and impressive piece of paperwork that you have seen? Did you learn something from it?

The work of Matt Shlian is incredible. His work is most certainly three-dimensional but in a more pristine and mathematical way. Although he doesn't use algorithms, his work looks almost computer-generated because of the perfection and purity it exudes. What I have learned is that paper art can come in so many immeasurable forms which all rely on our hands and creative minds. I become more and more amazed at what artists have made with paper because it is evolving and continuously growing.

Anemonae II

This all-white piece was a commission for an art collector. The inside of the work symbolizes the sea creatures found on the ocean floor. This piece looks very different when the lights are turned on and off, imitating the ocean's varying aesthetics between night and day.

Tools: *110 lb paper, knife, PVC glue, LED lights*
Techniques: *Cutting, bending, gluing*

Blue Mountains Majesty

The colors and forms of this large-scale piece are reminiscent of the Colombian mountains at dusk. The light coming from within can be switched on and off by the audience who will witness how the light changes the look and feel of the artwork.

Tools: *110 lb paper, knife, PVC glue, LED lights*
Techniques: *Cutting, bending, gluing*

Anther

In this piece, Sara kept the crude, raw color of the original paper which is not pure white. Although "Anther" has a simpler form and cut, it speaks volumes about shadows and layers.

Tools: *Craft knife with #11 blade, cotton paper, PVC glue*
Techniques: *Cutting, bending, gluing*

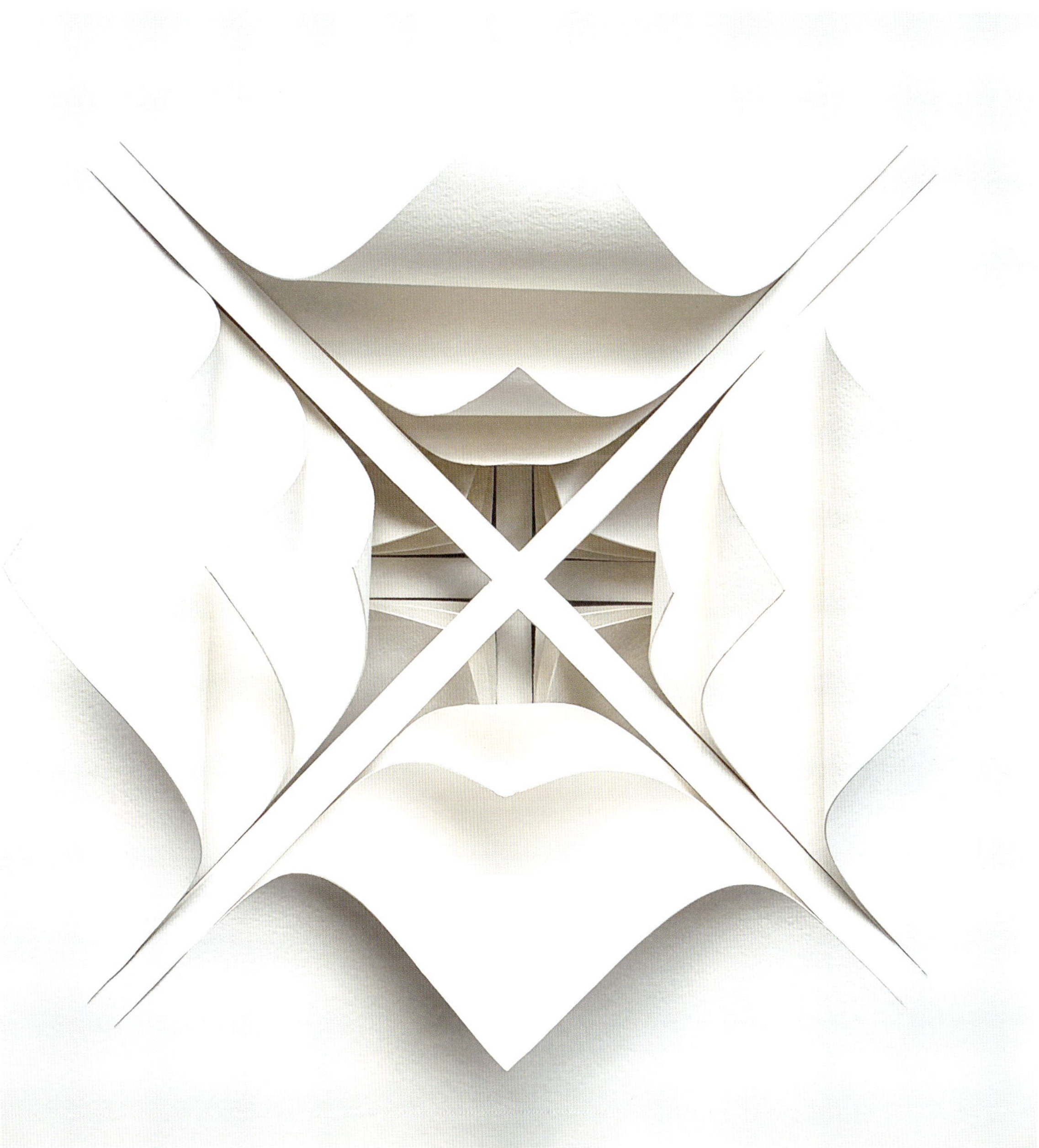

Dionaea

This piece was inspired by the plumage, leaves of the tropical flora, and fauna that abound in the tropics of Colombia. Birds sometimes resemble flowers or vice versa, and this is an homage to the beauty in nature on this planet and its incredible mystery. The bright red and interior blue provide a shocking contrast with the crude white that could either be a leaf or a feather of the flowers and birds that abound here.

Tools: *Acrylic paint, roller, craft knife with #11 blade, cotton paper, PVC glue*
Techniques: *Painting, cutting, bending, gluing*

Solaris II

It is a piece from a series of works based on the color yellow as well as our star of the solar system. This time, instead of the original white of the paper, all the surfaces were painted in harmonious colors.

Tools: *Acrylic paint, roller, craft knife with #11 blade, cotton paper, PVC glue*
Techniques: *Painting, cutting, bending, gluing*

Star-Spangled II

This piece is from Sara's spangled mountain series. She wanted to play with color and the raw freshness of the white surface to create forms inspired by stars as well as the color of the mountains in the evening which turn blue in Colombia.

Tools: *Acrylic paint, roller, craft knife with #11 blade, cotton paper, PVC glue*
Techniques: *Painting, cutting, bending, gluing*

Matt Shlian

"I often try to approach my work as a novice, to see endless possibilities in the creation of forms and their relationship with one another."

Matt Shlian is an artist, designer, and the founder of the Initiative Artist Studio in Ann Arbor, Michigan. By using his engineering skills to create kinetic sculpture, he extends his work from drawing to large-scale installation. Guided by curiosity, he makes paper artwork in order to understand it, enjoying the exploration of any possibilities of paper.

Unholy 79: Every Line is A Circle If You Make It Long Enough

This is 8 ft × 12 ft × 7 in sculpture was installed in the Tamarind Institute.

Tools: *PVA glue, spatulas, tweezers, awls*
Techniques: *Offset prints, folding, gluing*

Interview with **Matt Shlian**

When and how did you get involved in using paper to create art?

Originally I went to school for ceramics and felt interested in everything. I studied glass, painting, and so on. By the end, I had a dual major in ceramics and print media. However, I didn't make traditional ceramic or print work but created large digital prints and large-scale pop-up spreads by using a series of cut scores and creases. At that point, I was making some four-foot V-folds or strut fold pieces, hoping the work would be cohesive and interactive. One of my faculty advisers bought me pop-up books, and I started dissecting the paper pieces and figuring out how they worked. It took off from there.

Could you briefly describe your process of creating a piece of paper artwork?

My process is extremely varied from a piece-to-piece one. I often start without a clear goal in mind, working within a set of limitations. For example, in some pieces, I constrain myself to only use curved folds or make my lines in a specific length or angle. For some others, I begin with an idea of movement and try to achieve a particular shape or form somehow. Along the way, something usually goes wrong. However, a mistake sometimes becomes more interesting than the original idea, and then I continue with the work following the "mistake"—I enjoy being surprised.

Why do you prefer paper art?

There is an immediacy to paper. You may take a sheet and begin to work or plan something out methodically. It is a medium to preserve memory, a medium with which you can naturally create a dialog.

Most of your artworks involve geometric shapes. Why do you choose them as the dominant elements in your artworks?

I've always had an affinity for geometry. I am terrible at math, but I understand things spatially. Most of my work deals with the unfolding of space in one form or another. For instance, pieces in my "Ara" series are rooted in Arabic tiling. I want to create pieces that use geometric patterns, specifically patterns that are dissected and subsequently reconstructed. The work is not completely chaotic—there are moments where the underlying structure is visible—but overall the patterns are non-repeating.

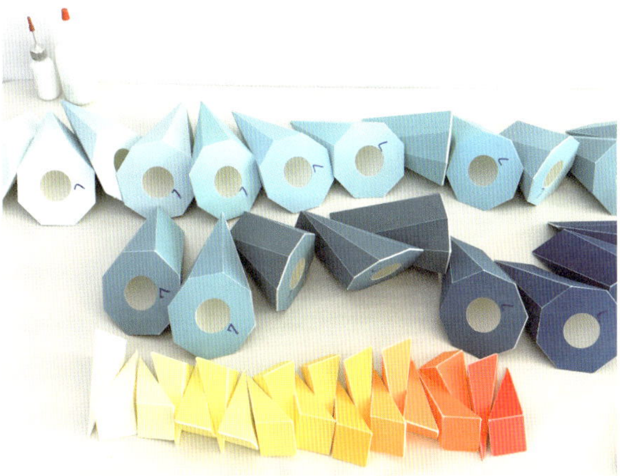

What do you want to express through your artworks?

Analyzing is more like the job of the viewer than the artist. I don't look at one specific thing and make a piece about it. My work is not didactic—I am not seeking to explain or present one specific idea in my pieces. Usually, I assume a viewer with limited knowledge of my work, process, or intent.

What is the biggest difference between your recent works and those you created at the beginning of your journey with paper art?

I think that the newer pieces are more refined and better crafted, but the early work was so fun and exploratory. Sometimes I try to use paper in a way that someone without experience might handle it. An unlearning process happens once you become too comfortable. I often try to approach my work as a novice, to see endless possibilities in the creation of forms and their relationship with one another. In this endeavor, I willfully forget what will work and why. This mindset allows me to evolve my visual language and discover new patterns.

Is there anything that you hope to improve? What do you plan to do?

I usually go too fast when making decisions in the studio. Sometimes I need to live with a piece for a while to make sense of it, which is hard to take time to do. To avoid getting impulsive, I need to work on slowing down.

Any suggestions for those who are just getting into paper art?

I don't have any specific advice. If I could go back to myself at 21 years old and tell myself something, I probably wouldn't say anything but to keep going. I tell my students to take time to develop what makes your work unique to you. How can you stand out? That only comes with time and struggle in your own work.

Unholy 220

Using iridescent paper, Matt created this 38 in × 48 in × 3 in sculpture.

Tools: *Iridescent paper, PVA glue, spatulas, tweezers, awls*
Techniques: *Folding, gluing*

Foreign Ministry 11

This sculpture is made out of paper with red and gold wash. The dimensions are: 31 in × 22.5 in × 1 in.

Tools: *PVA glue, spatulas, tweezers, awls*
Techniques: *Folding, gluing*

Omoplata

These four pieces are selected from Matt's "Omoplata" series which includes sculptures of different dimensions in various colors. The ones in vista iridescent blue and turquoise are Omoplata 11, the one in pear is 21, and the one in white is 27.

Tools: *PVA glue, spatulas, tweezers, awls*
Techniques: *Folding, gluing*

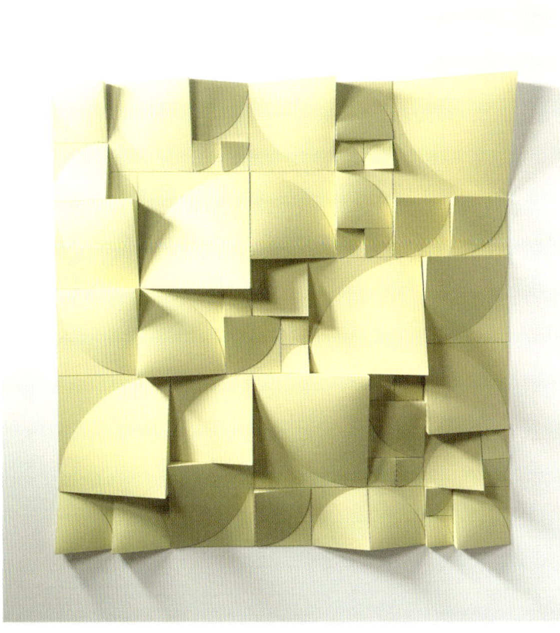

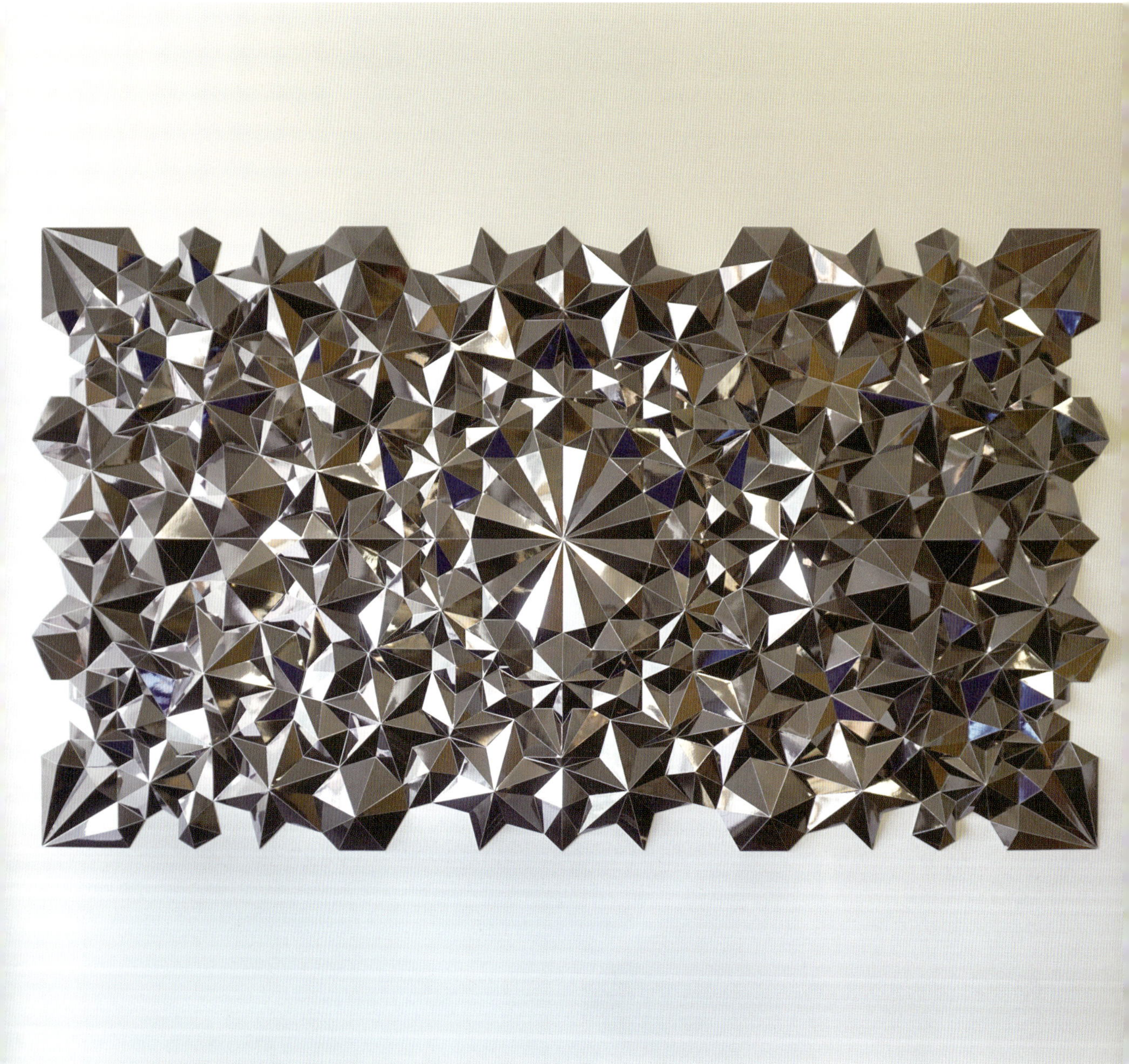

Ara 316: We Are Coming through the Windows If You Lock the Doors

Using gun-metal metallic paper, Matt created this 48 in × 76 in × 3 in sculpture.

Tools: *Gun-metal metallic paper*
Techniques: *Folding, gluing*

Woman

This is a collaborative work with the visual artist Brooke DiDonto who photographed the original picture in her "As Usual" series. Then Matt added a multitude of geometrical folds to the surface of it, giving the picture a bit of his style.

Tools: *PVA glue, spatulas, tweezers, awls*
Techniques: *Folding, gluing, archival print*

Cactus

Collaborating with Brooke DiDonto again, Matt curve folded an archival print to form this 8 in × 8 in × 8 in piece.

***Tools:** PVA glue, spatulas, tweezers, awls*
***Techniques:** Folding, archival print*

Ara 333

With the help of lithography, Matt created the gradient background for Ara 333 which was hollowed out of imperial blue paper. Its dimensions are 24 in × 24 in × 0.5 in.

Tools: *Imperial blue paper*
Technique: *Hollowing*

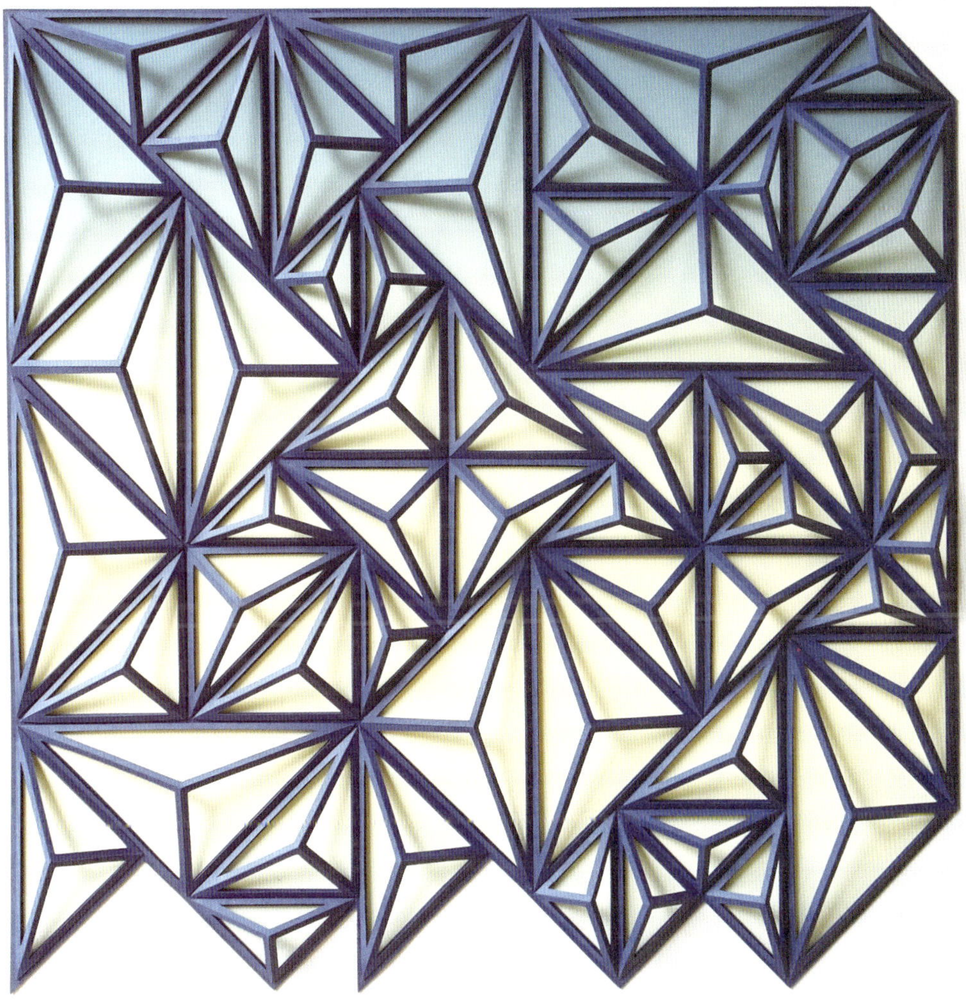

Zai Divecha

"I want my work to make people feel centered, quiet, and focused—a respite from an overstimulating world."

Zai Divecha is a paper sculpture artist living in San Francisco, California. By folding, pleating, or rolling sheets of white paper, she creates intricate patterns of light and shadow. Zai has shown at Marrow Gallery, West Coast Craft, and the American Craft Council and has been commissioned by Instagram, Twitter, and Square. (Portrait photo by Cassandra Jens, Pitaya Photography.)

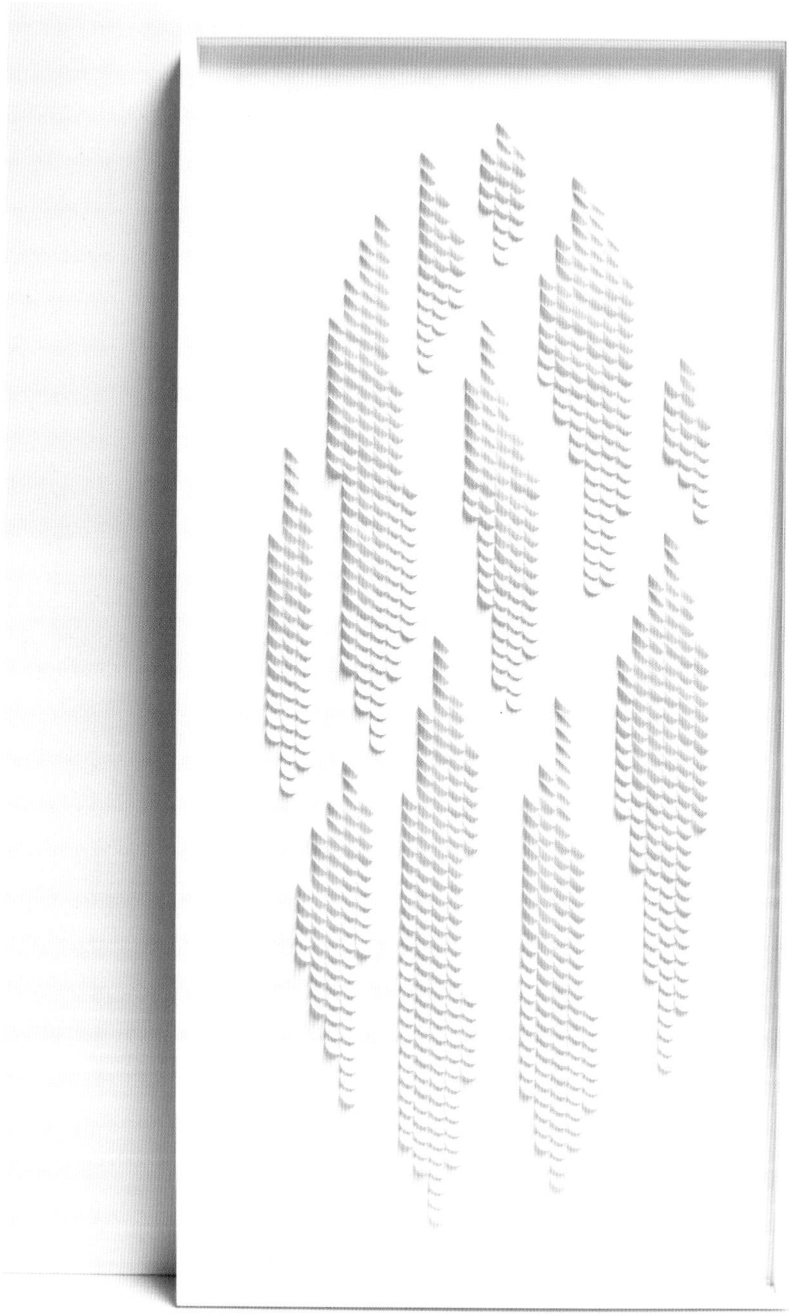

You Belong Here

"You Belong Here" was the 2012 slogan for AIDS/LifeCycle, an annual cycling event that raised money for HIV/AIDS organizations in California. The AIDS/LifeCycle community is tight-knit, joyful, and diverse. To Zai, this message is a reminder that there are many ways to work toward health justice—whether it's honoring a loved one, raising or giving money, or educating others.

Tools: *Adobe Illustrator, plotter cutter, glue*
Techniques: *Drawing, folding, gluing*

Interview with **Zai Divecha**

When and how did you start your journey of paper art?

I actually started out as a metalworker. A few years ago, my grandmother was hospitalized, and my family flew out to keep her company. To pass the time, I brought some paper, tools, and a book on making pop-up cards, thinking it might be a good creative exercise that I could apply to my metalworking. To my surprise, I fell in love with paper as a medium. It was easy to manipulate, and fast to prototype and iterate. Over the next year, I kept experimenting with paper, and dropped metalworking entirely.

Why is paper art special to you compared with other forms of art?

Paper is such an ordinary and unassuming material. We come into contact with it every day: We sign receipts, open envelopes, and jot down to-do lists. In these contexts, paper feels mundane and ephemeral. However, with just a few strategic and delicate alterations—a precise series of folds, or a collection of tiny cut flaps—I'm able to transform this familiar and expendable material into something totally different.

Where do you usually get inspiration?

I draw pattern inspiration from a variety of sources, both natural and human-made: bathroom tiles, clouds, storm drains, the "skeletons" of dead cactuses, peeling bark, raindrops on a car window, rock formations, and ornate screens in Islamic architecture.

Have you ever experienced a creative block? How did you overcome it?

For me, creativity is an ebb and flow. When I started working as a professional artist, the painter Susan Hall suggested that I cultivate a routine of making art—even if just for 30 minutes a day—whether or not I feel inspired. Gradually, I got used to putting in the work rather than waiting around for inspiration to strike. I wouldn't say my art practice is quite that routinized, but I do try to treat it more like a job than a passion.

Why do you prefer making all the paper artworks white?

I'm sensitive to my environment—sounds, smells, temperatures—and feel calmer and happier when "turning the volume down" on all kinds of sensory inputs. Therefore, I try to limit the amount of visual stimuli that I'm surrounded by. The all-white palette allows me to create patterns and texture with just light and shadow, which feels soothing. I want my work to make people feel centered, quiet and focused—a respite from an overstimulating world.

Many of your artworks are made of numbers of small pieces of geometric shapes. What does it take to develop these simple shapes into intricate and delicate artworks?

Repeating elements is really mesmerizing. On its own, a single tiny flap of paper isn't that interesting. However, if you cluster a lot of them together into a single composition, it takes on a completely different feeling. Typically, I create one "unit"—an incised flap, a pleated strip, or a rolled-up cone—and then repeat it dozens, hundreds, or thousands of times to compose a larger pattern. I try to balance geometric and organic elements in my work—the smallest units are often geometric and regular, while the overall composition is more organic and asymmetrical.

What is the biggest challenge you have experienced in your career as an artist?

Switching mediums from metal to paper was challenging, as I had built my entire art career and image around being a metalworker. I had to change not only my art practice but also my brand and people's impressions of my work. I knew in my heart that this was the right direction for me, but it felt a little scary to reinvent myself. I started sharing my experiments with paper on social media, and eventually people started to catch on. It takes time and courage to make big changes, but it's worth it.

Cumulus

Having scaled down her favorite pleat pattern to only a half-inch wide, Zai made this piece for a gallery show last year.

Tools: *Adobe Illustrator, plotter cutter*
Techniques: *Folding, gluing*

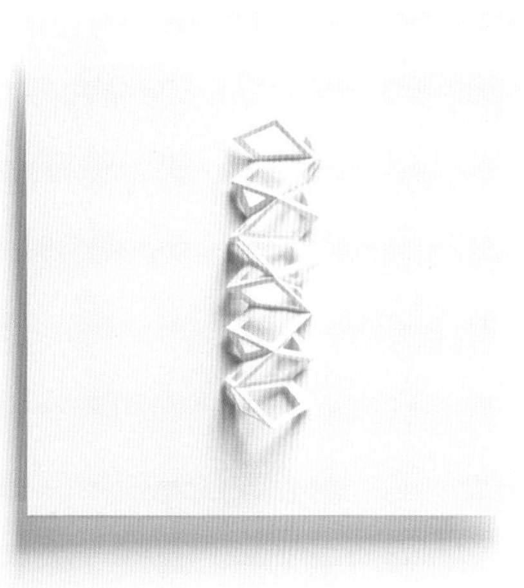

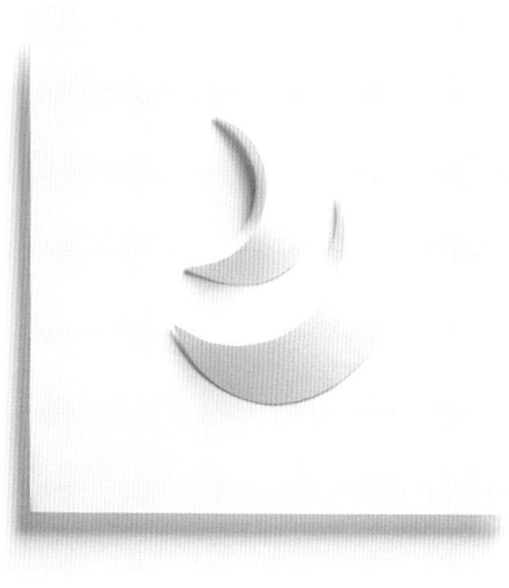

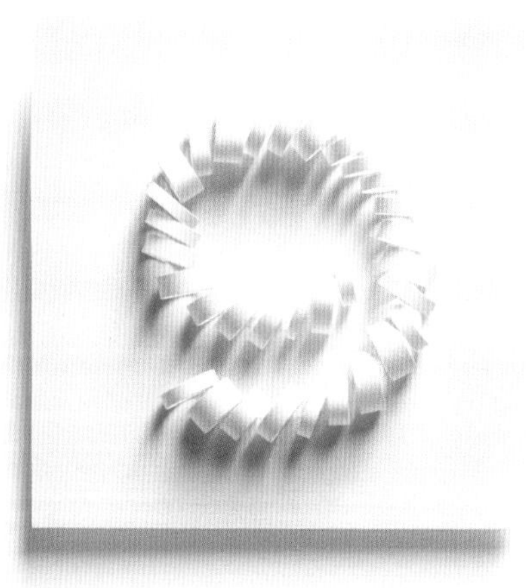

Quiet Type

In 2019, Zai participated in Adobe's 36 Days of Type, an annual global design challenge in which designers, illustrators, and artists create one letter of the alphabet and the digits zero through nine every day for 36 consecutive days. Each one of Zai's letters or numbers was created out of just paper and glue, and backed by a 5 in × 5 in sheet of paper.

Tools: *Adobe Illustrator, plotter cutter*
Techniques: *Folding, rolling, quilling, crumpling, poking holes, incising, gluing*

Torus

This piece uses a pleat pattern that can be widely seen in Zai's artwork. It is folded like an accordion and can be manipulated into curves or donut shapes.

Tools: *Adobe Illustrator, plotter cutter*
Techniques: *Folding, gluing*

Teardrops

This was a small study that Zai created as a prototype for her HIV/AIDS series.

Tools: *Adobe Illustrator, plotter cutter*
Technique: *Quilling*

INDEX

Ale Rambar

Costa Rica · Multi-Layered Paper Cutting

www.alerambar.com

P084–095

Diana Beltran Herrera

Colombia · Paper Sculpture

www.dianabeltranherrera.com

P160–169

Estudio Guardabosques

Argentina · Paper Sculpture

www.guardabosqu.es

P190–199

Hazel Glass

USA · Multi-Layered Paper Cutting

www.artbyhazelglass.com

P032–043

Héloïse Bossard

France · Paper Cutting

www.audetourdupapier.com

P044–051

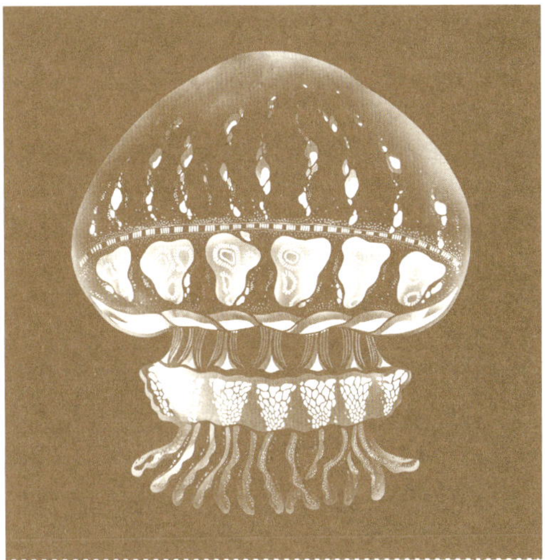

Jackie Wen

China · Paper Installation

www.instagram.com/jackie_wen

P170–177

JUDiTH+ROLFE

USA · On-Edge Paper / Quilling

www.judithandrolfe.com

P010–021

Makerie Studio

USA, UK, Norway · Paper Sculpture

www.makeriestudio.com

P132–141

María Laura Benavente Sovieri

Spain · Paper Sculpture

www.mililitros.com

P150–159

Marina Adamova

Russia · Paper Cutting / Type Design

www.talamaskanka.com

P064–073

Matt Shlian

USA · Paper Sculpture

www.mattshlian.com

P228–239

Owen Gildersleeve

UK · Paper Cutting / Illustration

www.owengildersleeve.com

P096–105

Pippa Dyrlaga

UK · Paper Cutting

www.pippadyrlaga.com

P052–063

Rosa Yoo

South Korea · Paper Sculpture

www.instagram.com/rosaiyoo

P200–209

Sam Pierpoint

UK · Paper Sculpture

www.sampierpoint.com

P210–217

Sara Rayo

Colombia · Paper Sculpture

www.pararayo.com

P218–227

Sarah Suplina

USA · Collage / Snippet

www.sarahsuplina.com

P114–121

Sena Runa

Portugal · Quilling

www.senaruna.com

P142–149

Shinobu Ohashi

Japan · Paper Cutting

www.ohashi-shinobu.com

P022–031

Sota

Japan · Paper Cutting

www.souta0521.com

P074–083

Tania Lissova

Russia · Paper Cutting / Collage

www.lissovacraft.etsy.com

P106–113

Yulia Brodskaya

UK · Quilling

www.artyulia.com

P122–131

Zai Divecha

USA · Paper Sculpture

www.zaidivecha.com

P240–248

Zim&Zou

France · Paper Installation

www.zimandzou.fr

P178–189

ACKNOWLEDGMENTS

We would like to express our gratitude to all of the artists and studios for their generous contribution of images, ideas, and concepts. We are also very grateful to many other people whose names do not appear in the credits, but who have made specific contributions and provided support. Without them, the successful compilation of this book would not have been possible. Special thanks to all of the contributors for sharing their innovation and creativity with all of our readers around the world.